Heaven Revealed

Heaven Revealed

The Holy Spirit and the Mass

David Bird OSB

GRACEWING

First published in 2008

Gracewing
2 Southern Avenue, Leominster
Herefordshire HR6 0QF

All rights reserved. No part of this publication may be reproduced, stored in a retrieval system, or transmitted in any form, or by any means, electronic, mechanical, photocopying, recording or otherwise, without the written permission of the publisher.

© David Bird, OSB 2008

The right of David Bird to be identified as the author of this work has been asserted in accordance with the Copyright, Designs and Patents Act 1988.

ISBN 978 0 85244 179 4

Typeset by Action Publishing Technology Ltd,
Gloucester GL1 5SR

After this I looked, and there in heaven a door stood open! ...
At once I was in the Spirit, and there in heaven stood a
throne, with one seated on the throne ...
And the four living creatures, ... day and night without
ceasing, sing
Holy, holy, holy, the Lord God the Almighty,
Who was and is and is to come.

Rev. 4:1–8

We knew not whether we were in heaven or on earth,
We only know that there God dwells among men.

*Envoys describing to Prince Vladimir of Kiev
the Eucharist celebrated in Byzantium*

At the centre of the Church is the Eucharist,
where Christ is present and active
in humanity and in the whole world
by means of the Holy Spirit.

Pope John Paul II

Contents

		Page
Foreword *by The Right Reverend Paul Stonham OSB* Abbot of Belmont		ix
Preface		xi

Part One: Principles

Prologue	Discerning the Truth	1
Chapter One	The Christian Mystery	9
Chapter Two	The Role of the Spirit in the Christian Mystery	18
Chapter Three	More Ways than One	40
Chapter Four	God is with us in Christ	49
Chapter Five	Ascent and Transformation	58
Chapter Six	The Twofold Gift of the Spirit	65
Chapter Seven	Epiclesis	78
Chapter Eight	Sacrifice, our Way to God	95
Chapter Nine	The Mass and the Martyrs	105

Part Two: Practice

Chapter Ten	Celebrating	115
Chapter Eleven	Variety in Unity	125
Chapter Twelve	The Liturgy of Life	129
Chapter Thirteen	*Lectio Divina*	135
Chapter Fourteen	The Bread of the Presence	145
Chapter Fifteen	Images	152
Epilogue		163

Foreword

On the feast of the Transfiguration 1981, three monks of Belmont Abbey, England, arrived in Lima on the final stage of their journey to found a Benedictine monastery in the desert of northern Peru. Such an enterprise could only survive and flourish if it were the work of the Holy Spirit. Although two of the monks eventually returned to the United Kingdom, Fr Luke Waring after nine and the writer of this introduction after twenty happy years in Peru, Fr David Bird still lives in the Monastery of the Incarnation, now in its new home at Pachacmac, about an hour's drive south of Lima.

This book, Fr David's third, is the fruit of fifty years' monastic life in Europe and Latin America. In it we discover the author's profound knowledge of the Scriptures, the Fathers and the Monastic Tradition. At the same time on every page we find his love for the living Church, at first through his work as teacher and spiritual director at Belmont Abbey School, which sadly closed in 1994, then as assistant pastor in Herefordshire, West Cumbria and Tambogrande, and finally as parish priest in Piura, Negritos and San Miguel. He shares his experiences with his readers, distilled, as it were, through the eyes and heart of a monk, a scholar and a contemplative, for Fr David is truly a man of God.

Central to the monastic life is the daily celebration of the Eucharist, through which the Church is nourished and nurtured by word and sacrament. The monk's hope and prayer, the focus of his contemplation, is the coming of the Kingdom in the person of Christ. He prays that by doing God's will on earth, all men and women will come to catch a glimpse even now, in this vale of tears, a glimpse of heaven – heaven revealed. A monastery, if nothing else, must be a little bit of heaven here on earth, a place where both monks and guests can experience God's love and where, in the words of St Augustine, we can enjoy God.

In the third Eucharist Prayer we ask the Father to make holy our gifts of bread and wine that by the power of the Holy Spirit they may become the Body and Blood of Christ. We go on to pray that, nourished by that Body and Blood, we may be filled with the Holy Spirit and become one Body, one Spirit in Christ. It is the Eucharist which makes us the Body of Christ and Temple of the Holy Spirit. It is the Eucharist that reveals to us our true identity. It is the Eucharist that sanctifies us or, as the Fathers would say, divinizes us, makes us what we were created to be, daughters and sons of God.

In this new book Fr David presents us with his insights into the Eucharist as the work of the Holy Spirit. It is the Spirit who makes Christ present within and among us, a presence that heralds the coming of the Kingdom of God, a Kingdom which is none other than Jesus Christ himself, the Son of the Living God, our Lord and Saviour.

It gives me great pleasure to introduce this book to you. May it strengthen your faith and fill you with joy.

Dom Paul Stonham
Abbot of Belmont

Preface

When God became man in Jesus Christ he ended a controversy that had been fought out in the pages of the Old Testament. In Exodus, it says that God was visible on Mount Sinai, not only to Moses, but also to some of the leaders of the people (Exod. 24:9–11), while in Deuteronomy (4:12–20), great emphasis is put on the assertion that the people could not see God, and this is linked with the prohibition of any form of image. However, with Christ, God has a human face and has become a human being, a part of our history, and 'Whoever has seen me has seen the Father.' (John 14:8–10).

In the Gospels, there is a strong visual element in God's revelation of himself in Christ. This was specially so for the Synoptic Gospels in the Transfiguration (Matt. 17:1–13; Mark 9:2–13; Luke 9:28–36), and for St John, in Christ's passion and death. 'Glory' is the manifestation of God's presence; and in St John's Gospel, both the Father and Christ are 'glorified' in Christ's death on the cross because it is the supreme revelation of God and of Christ as Self-giving Love. The supreme revelation of God for us is not a teaching but a scene of execution and death painted in words; and whoever believes in him who was crucified and was lifted up will have eternal life (John 3:4–5).

This visual aspect of God making contact with the human race continues to the present day through the Church which is Christ's body, his physical and hence visible presence on earth. The Church makes Christ visible to the world through its unity (John 17:23) and the quality of its love; and Christ becomes invisible when the Church and Christians fail to love. When the Church defends itself as a human institution, but to the neglect of charity and truth, it can only create scandal; but when it loves as Christ loves, then it is fulfilling its function as the body of Christ. It is as true for the Church as a whole as it is for individual Christians that 'Those who find their life will lose it, and those who lose their life for my sake will find it' (Matt. 10:39). In the words of Charles de Foucauld, we must 'Cry out the Gospel with our lives'. But this can only happen in so far as we share in the Christian Mystery as deeply and as authentically as possible; and this sharing also has its visual element.

When this element is neglected, Christian revelation can be smothered in its own words, especially in the modern world where their meaning and importance can be hidden among the sheer volume of other words that clamour for our attention and assail our ears from all sides, almost all the time. The only thing that distinguishes Christian words from other words is sanctity; and sanctity depends, not on us nor on the words by themselves, but on the presence of God. It is our function to manifest the presence of God in our liturgy, by the quality of our lives, and in all aspects of Church life. God must increase and we must decrease, even liturgically, and this can happen only through the Holy Spirit.

It is the Holy Spirit who turns a collection of texts into the word of God, a meal into the Eucharist, a gathering of people into the body of Christ, a sinner into a son or daughter of God, a painting into an icon, the prayers of people on earth into the prayers of Christ in heaven. It is the Holy Spirit who bridges time, space and eternity, and hence has made possible both the Incarnation, with its links to all humanity, and the Church which is the visible part of the gathering in Christ of all the redeemed, past, present and future, in heaven, on earth and anywhere in between. Central to all these functions of the Holy Spirit is the Eucharist by which the Church is shown to be the body of Christ: and Christ is in heaven: hence the title of this book.

This book was written during the second half of 2006 when I was *padre formador*, spiritual director, in the 'Jesus Vive' community, seminarians belonging to the Charismatic Renewal who wish to eventually become a religious community. I want to thank all the members of that community for their kindness and support during the writing of this book. I also wish to thank my abbot, Fr Paul Stonham, for his support by internet, for writing the Introduction, and for lending me to the 'Jesus Vive' community. I also want to record my gratitude to Brother Alex Echeandia who, together with Fr Dyfrig Harris at Belmont, has taught me all I know about icons. Finally, my thanks go to Dr Richard Lennan, an Australian theologian who is now doing a sabbatical in Washington DC, who kindly revised the manuscript. He did the job very thoroughly and wisely; and this book owes much to his very constructive criticism.

I must acknowledge my debt to Olivier Clément in his book *The Roots of Christian Mysticism*, who has given me almost all my patristic quotations; to Bishop Hilarion Alfeyev of the Russian Orthodox Church for his book *St Symeon the New Theologian and Orthodox Tradition*; to Archbishop John Zizioulas of the Greek Orthodox Church for his book *Being as Communion*; to Fr Alexander Schmemann for his books, *The Eucharist* and *The World As Sacrament*; to Vladimir Lossky for his classic *The Mystical Theology of the Eastern Church*; and to Fr John Meyendorff for his book *A Study of Gregory Palamas*. I am also indebted to Narciso Jesus Lorenzo Leal for his thesis on '*La Epiclesis y La Divinizacion del Hombre*' which he defended in the University of Salamanca and published in *Nova et Vetera*, of the Monasterio de Benedictinas, Zamorra, Spain. I have used this extensively in the chapter on the Epiclesis. Also, I have learned much from and used *The Theology of*

Joseph Ratzinger by Aidan Nichols OP, who is now John Paul II Lecturer in Theology at Oxford; as also from *Catholicism* by Henri de Lubac; from an article 'The Idea of the Church: Abbot Butler and Vatican II' by Fr Paul McPartlan in the *Downside Review* of January 2003; from *Theology at the Eucharistic Table* by Jeremy Driscoll OSB; and from *The Christian Universe* by E. L. Mascall. All Scripture quotations are from the *New Revised Standard Version*.

This book is more a by-product of my monastic life than a work of scholarship, so there is more of me in it than is usual in a really scientific work; but most of the Fathers who have contributed to the Tradition in which I write were not scholars either. However, I hope it stands the test of scholarly scrutiny; which is why I asked Dr Richard Lennan to read and criticize it before offering it for publication. For the same reason, I could think of none better than my abbot, Fr Paul Stonham, to write the Foreword. He speaks Greek, is well acquainted with Orthodoxy, passed some time on Mount Athos as a young man, and only recently prayed in the cave of St Gregory Palamas. We also shared twenty years together in Peru, until he was elected Abbot of Belmont. I am still there as a monk of Pachacamac, south of Lima, Peru, a monastery he founded. Both of us are intent on drawing from both Western and Eastern sources in our spiritual life, attempting to unite in ourselves the two traditions while remaining resolutely Western Catholics. This is not too difficult a task for Benedictines. How useful it is, you can judge for yourselves.

Prologue

Disclosing the Truth

If I ever had to show someone what Catholicism is about in a short period of time, I would take them to Lourdes. Large numbers of people from every country under the sun, of every condition of life, rich and poor, clergy and lay people, young and old, the healthy and the sick, come together for a common purpose. Through participating in the pilgrimage, a greater and higher truth can be discerned and experienced and, when that happens, it cannot fail to inspire. The Mass at Lourdes is a celebration of variety realizing unity, and people collect under their different banners and sing in their different languages, do their different things, and experience and manifest their active membership of one single body, the Church.. They are so united to Christ that they are truly children of Our Lady and brothers and sisters of one another. As St Maximos the Confessor wrote,

> Men, women, children, deeply divided as to race, nationality, language, class, work, knowledge, rank and fortune ... are all created afresh by the Church in the Spirit. On all alike she impresses a divine form ... Therefore all are united in a truly catholic way. In the Church no one is in any way separated from the community. Everyone is, so to speak, merged into everyone else by the simple and indivisible power of faith ... Christ is thus everything in everyone, Christ who incorporates everything in himself.

That is the vision that is experienced at Lourdes; and it is also a place where lay people can be seen to take on their proper role as members of the Church, co-responsible under Christ with the clergy for the good of the whole enterprise. When I taught at Belmont Abbey School and went on pilgrimage to Lourdes with the boys, we used to take our tents to the scout camp on the hill and, when the opportunity offered, we used to help with the sick. In this way, the boys received an insight into what being a Catholic involves, through the experience of devotion, sacrifice and fun which is a Lourdes pilgrimage. Once, practically all the rule-breakers and rebels of the school signed on. 'You must be mad to take that lot,' said the headmaster. Actually, they formed a very good group. Many years later, when they were mostly married and settled, I met the mother of one of them who told me that her son was a very keen and committed Catholic. 'His attitude to religion changed when he went with you to Lourdes,' she said, 'and it has lasted till now.' I never noticed it at the time.

Lourdes is quite clearly a place of vision, of charity, of hope, even of miracle; and people can explore it and share in it simply by taking part. Any practices, like solemn Masses, long processions, rosaries and queues, that would be highly inconvenient and even unacceptable in normal life, make sense in this context.

Another place where young people and others are free to discover the Gospel through living it together with others is Taizé, six kilometres from the historic ruins of Cluny in Burgundy. It is an ecumenical monastic community with members from different churches, including Catholics. Now it receives around 6,000 young people every week and 100,000 pilgrims every year from every part of the world. So much for secularism: when the Gospel is manifested by people's lives in an appropriate setting and young people are free to explore without pressure, anything can happen. Taizé is another place of vision, that of its founder, the late Brother Roger Schutz.

It is a place of reconciliation and unity in love. People can enter into that vision without being preached at or having answers imposed on them from outside: the answers they are looking for are glimpsed at through the common life of Taizé. The prayer sessions three times a day, the lack of comfort and the meagre meals are acceptable to young people, even to those who have little to do with their home parish, because they are part of what it takes to go on exploring. People go to places like Lourdes and Taizé and, hopefully, bring the vision home with them. To make an impact we need more places where Christian truth can be glimpsed through the facts on the ground. Such places are hard to come by in a secular world.

Big events, like World Youth Day which Pope John Paul II used to attend to great effect and which the present Pope Benedict XVI also attended in Cologne with a very different but equally effective manner, are also moments of vision, and people come in their millions. Moreover, millions glimpsed the Gospel in the life of Mother Teresa and in the almost public death of Pope John Paul II.

When I became parish priest of Negritos in northern Peru, there was a different approach to membership of the parish from any I had experienced, and this showed in the nearest thing to a youth club that we had. Although there are obviously exceptions, most people who consider themselves members of the parish belong to one of the groups that contribute in some way to the purposes of the parish; and the parish has a communal mission and sense of purpose beyond its mere continued existence or its observance of the rules of the Church. First Communion is at the end of primary school, and Confirmation at the end of secondary school, and both sacraments are preceded by a two-year preparation. By the time of Confirmation, some are already altar servers or members of the choir, but the last meetings of preparation are taken up by discussions concerning the concrete steps they can take to exercise their roles as fully-adult members of the Catholic community. There is a variety of activities in the parish, so they have a wide choice, and it has been known for young people to invent their own ministry. A room in the parish hall is reserved for active members of the parish youth to hold their meetings and relax; and members have a sense of purpose beyond simply playing billiards, because they know they are an active part of the body of Christ in Negritos. They can see the doctrine in the facts of parochial life; and the facts, the discussions and the prayers lead them to glimpse the transcendent truth.

Negritos is a petroleum town where people came in the pursuit of jobs and money. Thirty years ago, the parish was almost dead because people had lost the Christian customs of their places of origin, and their ambitions and interests were all bound up with the petroleum industry. Then the Charismatic Renewal arrived. Its message struck home; and the first meetings had to be held in the sports complex because there was not enough room in the church. Negritos had become a parish with vision; and this has not been lost but has developed, matured and deepened over the years.

Christian life in common, in whatever shape it comes, is meant to be a vision, an icon of the truth of Christ for the world, whether we are talking of permanent communities like the universal Church, the diocese, the Christian family, the parish or a monastery, or events where Christians come together for some specific reason. This is what Jesus means when he says in John 17:21 that the special kind of loving unity among Christians will lead the world to accept that he has been sent by the Father; they will glimpse a little of the life of the Trinity in the common life of the Church.

Because of the Incarnation, Christian revelation has a visual dimension. Many have desired to see the things we see, and have not seen them. As St Francis of Assisi said, 'Believers see and believe: non-believers just see.' Where there is vision, both in life and in liturgy, there is growth.

Where there is no vision, when the facts on the ground do not require faith to make sense of them and do not invite us to explore, savour and participate in the Christian Mystery through them, there is stagnation and many fall away. We must all recapture the vision of what it means to be a Catholic, not in a xenophobic way, but in the joy of the Spirit; and we must express it clearly in our lives, our liturgy and our activity. It is only in that way that the modern world will *see* the truth of Christianity as Christ teaches us in St John's Gospel. The challenge is ours, but the power to do it comes from the Holy Spirit; so let us not shame him by believing it to be impossible.

Where better to start than with the Mass? – which is both the source and the summit of everything else that Catholics believe and do. How can the liturgy of the Mass best reflect the Christian Mystery which it celebrates? How can we impart a vision, a glimpse of the reality which is the whole reason why we go to Mass on Sundays? When the Prince Vladimir of Kiev wanted missionaries to evangelize his people, he sent emissaries to all the centres of Christianity to find out who would render a better service. Those who returned from Constantinople were completely in awe about what they experienced in the Eucharist that was celebrated there:

> We knew not whether we were in heaven or on earth, for surely there is no such splendour or beauty anywhere on earth. We cannot describe it to you; we only know that God dwells there among men and that their Service surpasses the worship of all other places ...

This is the reason why Russia is an Orthodox country. The liturgy that was developed after Vatican II has not yet reached its full potential or definitive form, nor has it had the effect on many people that we hoped it would have had when it first came out. One investigation found that only 29 per cent of American Catholics believe in the

Real Presence. If the changes had been all that successful, the people should have a clearer insight into the Real Presence than before the changes. I am not advocating a return to the past, but a compelling vision for the future expressed in an equally compelling liturgy. I hope this book will contribute something to the liturgy's further development.

Part One
Principles

Chapter One

The Christian Mystery

Christianity is not a 'religion' or a confession in the way the last three hundred years would have understood the word: a system of more or less dogmatically certain truths to be accepted and confessed, and of moral commands to be observed or at least accorded recognition. Both elements, intellectual structure and moral law, belong, of course, to Christianity; but neither exhausts its essence. Still less is Christianity a matter of religious sentiment, a more or less emotionally-toned attitude towards 'the divine', which binds itself to no dogmatic or moral system whatever. St Paul thinks of Christianity, the good news, as a 'mystery'; but not merely in the sense of a hidden, mysterious teaching about the things of God ... Rather for him *mysterium* means first of all a deed of God's, the execution of an everlasting plan of his through an act which proceeds from his eternity, realized in time and the world, and returning once more to him its goal in eternity. We can express the mystery, so conceived, by the one word 'Christ', meaning by it the Saviour's person together with his mystical body, the Church. It embraces first of all [God's] Incarnation ... planning of salvation ... bearing the burden of [man's] sin ... the cross and death ... [and finally] Everything ... must bend the

knee before the name of Jesus'.
Odo Casel OSB, *The Mystery of Christian Worship*[1]

It is he who endured every kind of suffering in all those who foreshadowed him. In Abel he was slain, in Isaac bound, in Jacob exiled, in Joseph sold, in Moses exposed to die. He was sacrificed in the Passover lamb, persecuted in David, dishonoured in the prophets.
It is he who was made man of the Virgin, he who was hung on a tree, it is he who was buried in the earth, raised from the dead, and taken up to the heights of heaven.
The type has passed away; the reality has come. The lamb gives place to God; the sheep gives place to a man; and the man is Christ, who fills the whole of creation.
Saint Melito of Sardis (second century)[2]

Christ is the great hidden mystery, the blessed goal, the purpose for which everything was created ... with his gaze fixed on this goal God called things into existence. He [Christ] is the point to which Providence is tending ... He is the mystery which surrounds all ages ... In fact it is for the sake of Christ and for his mystery, that all ages exist and all that they contain. In Christ they have received their principle and their purpose. This synthesis was predetermined at the beginning: a synthesis of the limit and the unlimited, of the measured and the immeasurable, of the bounded and the boundless, of the Creator and the creature, of rest and movement. In the fullness of time the synthesis became visible in Christ, and God's plans were fulfilled.
St Maximos the Confessor (seventh century)[3]

If the Liturgy is, in the words of Pope Pius XI, the main vehicle of the ordinary magisterium of the Church, it is not, in the first place, because of the authority of those who composed it or ratified it, but because of the active presence of the Holy Spirit who makes Christ present in the Christian community. By the power of the Spirit, Christ speaks through the readings, presides through the priest, exhorts through the sermon, and sings and prays through the hymns and prayers of the community, illuminating the minds of those taking part in accordance with their faith. In the liturgy the Church is in touch with the Reality behind its faith in an unprecedented manner, and for this reason liturgy is the proper context for understanding the Christian Mystery in which the faithful are participating. This is stated in the Latin adage *Lex orandi lex credendi*: the law of prayer is the law of belief. It is within the context of the Father sending the Spirit (Pentecost and the *epiclesis* of the Mass) to make us one body with Christ, and the Spirit uniting us to Christ in our ascent to the Father in praise (the *doxology* at the end of the Eucharistic Prayer), that the New Testament was written and Catholic understanding of it brought about. All aspects and dimensions of the relationship which the Church has with God come together in the Eucharistic celebration and are there experienced as an organic whole by the Church. This is in accordance with the patristic vision of the Church. Cardinal Newman wrote:

> It is the great evidence of truth, in the case of revealed teaching, that it is so consistent, that it so hangs together, that one thing springs out of another, that each part requires and is required by the rest. The great truths of Revelation are all connected together and form a whole. To understand the full consistency and harmony of Catholic teaching requires study and meditation. Hence, as philosophers of this world bury themselves in museums and laboratories, descend into mines, or wander among woods or on the sea shore, so the enquirer into heavenly truths dwells in the cell and the oratory, pouring forth his heart in prayer, collect-

ing his thoughts in meditation ... till before his mental sight arises the hidden wisdom of the perfect, 'which God predestined before the world unto his glory'.[4]

People becoming Catholics or returning to the Church are required to accept the whole package, lock, stock and barrel, and not to pick and choose between doctrines or try to add or subtract anything of their own. Cardinal Newman said that the Church, in defining its different doctrines down the ages, was only defining one thing. Theology has to separate and analyse in order to understand, and we get used to the separate chapters or books on different doctrines and different kinds of theology; but the liturgical experience of the Church makes it clear that the wonderful deeds of God in Christ, the Christian life we live and the different doctrines we believe in are all organically united to each other in one Christian Mystery. To study, analyse, and to discover new or forgotten aspects of theological truths in their separateness is the function of scholarship. To proclaim and expound the Christian Mystery as a whole, and to discern and judge theological work in relation to that Mystery are the functions of the Episcopate, because it is the bishop who presides at the liturgy in which the Christian Mystery is celebrated. Christian scholarship needs brains, method and humility; to enter into the Christian Mystery we need purity of heart, openness to Catholic Tradition and to the Holy Spirit.

We enter this Mystery at Baptism and celebrate it in the Mass. To separate doctrines permanently from their source and context in the Christian Mystery is to hide their true importance, to diminish them, to cease properly to understand them, and to open up the way to a 'pick-and-choose' kind of Christianity that is a ghost of its former self. To deny one doctrine puts our acceptance of the rest in jeopardy, while to accept one doctrine can be the first step towards accepting the whole of Catholic truth. Thus, Cardinal Newman wrote:

You must accept the whole or reject the whole; attenuation does but enfeeble, and amputation mutilate. It is trifling to receive all but something which is as integral as any other portion; and, on the other hand, it is a solemn thing to accept any part, for, before you know where you are, you may be carried on by a stern logical necessity to accept the whole.[5]

Both processes are alive and well in the Anglican Church. Hence we have the well-rounded Christian holiness of many people in Anglican history like Lancelot Andrews, Bishop Ken, John Wesley, John Keble etc, and there is the wonderful theology of John H. Newman before his conversion, the sane and balanced Christian understanding in recent times of C. S. Lewis, of Austin Farrer, Eric Mascall and John Macquarrie, of Archbishop Michael Ramsey who anticipated much of Vatican II before it ever met, and of Rowan Williams, the present Archbishop of Canterbury. The other tendency is amply illustrated in the liberal literature in which Jesus is not incarnate and Christianity is just one religion among others, and people are told to pick and choose what doctrines they accept and what doctrines they reject. It is too easy to become post-Christians while still managing to dress up like the real thing.

The Scriptures are historical documents like any other, and at the same time the Word of God. These two dimensions of Sacred Scripture are essential to one another, distinct without being separate. As historical documents, they belong to the times in which they were written, and, if the historical dimension were the only one, their message would be only as certain as are the opinions of their expert interpreters. However, they are also the Word of God, a vehicle by which the Father speaks to us down the ages through Christ in the power of the Spirit, forming a continuous dialogue between himself and the Church, which is the New Covenant at work. Here we remember the words of Origen:

> We are said to drink the blood of Christ not only when we receive it according to the rite of the mysteries, but also when we receive his words, in which life dwells, as he said himself, 'the words I have spoken to you are spirit and life.' (John 6:63)[6]

As historical documents, the interpretation of Scripture depends on the expertise of scholars: as Word of God it depends on clarity of vision which, in turn, depends on the presence of the Holy Spirit filling a pure heart; and the saints down the ages are the group most qualified to understand the Word of God, like the disciple whom Jesus loved on whom St Peter relied to find out the meaning of Christ's words (John 13:21-6). There is a parallel with Christ. If modern scientists had met Christ two thousand years ago, they could have studied his body fruitfully with all the means open to them; but they would never have discovered the most important thing about him, that he was the Word made flesh. That truth can only be reached through faith. Likewise, the most important thing about Scripture is that it is the Word of God; and this can only be discovered by faith. Thus, the laboratory and the university are proper places for studying the Scriptures as historical documents; but this can only take us so far. Such a study by itself can produce, at best, only second-hand theology. It needs to be complemented by the knowledge that comes from prayerful reading, especially in the liturgical assembly where those who read, those who listen, and all who respond in prayer and sacrifice are united to Christ in the Church by the Spirit.

If the university is the proper place to reach an understanding of the Scriptures as historical documents, the proper places for reaching an understanding of the Word of God are, in J. H. Newman's words, the oratory for the liturgy and the cell for private reading, both in a context of prayer. As St Isaac of Nineveh wrote, 'Reckon prayer to be the key that opens the true meaning of the Scriptures.'

Obviously both scientific study and prayerful insight in

communion with the Church are gifts from God, and the best theologians combine them. Nevertheless, only Scripture as the Word of God can lead us into the Christian Mystery. As St Ambrose put it, when we read or listen to Sacred Scripture, God speaks to us; and when we pray, we speak to God. We are participants in a dialogue that is brought about by the Holy Spirit between God and the Church; and hence, to take part in this dialogue we need to be mentally in communion with the Church. Although it continues outside the liturgy in the prayerful reading of Scripture – what we call *lectio divina* – and in devotion to the Blessed Sacrament and in the use of icons – its centre is the Eucharistic Assembly. By prayerfully reading Scripture with the mind of the Church, we are led by the Holy Spirit into the Christian Mystery where we touch the reality about which Scripture speaks, entering into communion with Christ.

If the Christian Mystery forms an organic whole it is because of the presence of the Holy Spirit who binds it together. Leave out the Spirit, and the relationship between the events of Our Lord's life, death and resurrection, the word and sacraments, the Bible and Tradition, heaven and earth, our Christian lives and the Eucharist, the doctrines of the Church, its authority and our spiritual life, is obscured or becomes invisible. Dogmas become mere rules to control the way we think, and the only obstacle between us and a pick-and-choose form of Christianity becomes what the Pope will 'allow'. The end result is that our understanding becomes limited by our own horizons and distorted by our sinfulness and lack of faith. With the Holy Spirit everything is interconnected and understood in relationship to everything else, which means it is understood in its proper context in the Christian Mystery: without the Holy Spirit we see the truths of faith only from the outside and come to mistake them for mere opinions.

Rowan Williams, the Archbishop of Canterbury, has a moving meditation on an icon of the Transfiguration which, perhaps better than words, depicts something of the Christian Mystery. It reveals Christ as the centre of all history and of every personal biography. It shows us that everything is connected to him and will only be truly understood when that connection has been revealed:

> The dark background against which Jesus is shown is something you will see in other icons as a way of representing the depths of heavenly reality. In the transfiguration, what the disciples see is, as you might say, Jesus' humanity 'opening up' to its inner dimensions ... So the disciples look at Jesus and see him as *coming out* from an immeasurable depth; behind or within him, infinity opens up, the 'dwelling of the light', to borrow the haunting phrase from Job 38:19 ... John's Gospel too uses the language of 'coming out' from the depths of the Father (John 16:27–30). Belief in Jesus is seeing him as the gateway to an endless journey into God's love ... The whole history of God's dealings with his people is involved in this; Moses and Elijah are also driven towards us by the same energy. But Jesus alone stands in the very heart of it, it flows in him and from him. It is the light from him that is reflected on the robes of his companions. They lived hundreds of years before him, yet what makes them radiant, what makes them agents of God, is the light coming from Jesus, so this icon – like the story it illustrates – confuses our ordinary sense of time ... In Jesus, the world of ordinary prosaic time is not destroyed, but it is broken up and reconnected, it works no longer just in straight lines but in layers and spirals of meaning. We begin to understand how our lives, like those of Moses and Elijah, may have meanings we can't know of in this present moment: the real depth and significance of what we say or do now won't appear until more of the light of Christ has been seen. And so what we think is crucially important may not be so; what we think insignificant may be what truly changes us for good or

evil. Christ's light alone will make the final pattern coherent, for each one of us as for all human history.[7]

Meanwhile, we celebrate this Christian Mystery that, through the Holy Spirit, embraces all reality, past, present and future, and relates it to Christ. Through Christ, God's love pours into all creation; and we hear his word and bow in adoration as he, the key to all history, manifests himself by giving himself to us as food and drink.

Notes

1 Odo Casel OSB, *The Mystery of Christian Worship* (DLT, 1962), pp. 9–11.
2 *Sources Chrétiennes* 123, 65–71.
3 *Questions to Thalassios*, 60 (*PG* 90, 612), taken from Oliver Clément, *The Roots of Christian Mysticism* (New City, 1993), p. 39.
4 Cardinal J. H. Newman, *Discourses to Mixed Congregations*, pp. 343, 360–1.
5 Newman, *Essay on the Development of Docrine*, p. 94.
6 Origen, *Homilies on Numbers* 16.9 *PG* 12, 701 (taken from Clément, *Roots*, p. 97).
7 Rowan Williams, *The Dwelling of the Light* (Canterbury Press, Norwich, 2003), p. 4ff.

Chapter Two

The Role of the Spirit in the Christian Mystery

> The Holy Spirit will come upon you
> and the power of the Most High will overshadow you;
> therefore the child to be born will be holy;
> he will be called
> Son of God.
>
> Luke 1:35

> And the Word became flesh and lived among us.
>
> John 1:14

> How much more will the blood of Christ,
> who through the eternal Spirit
> offered himself without blemish to God,
> purify our conscience from dead works to worship
> the living God.
>
> Heb. 9:14

> If the Spirit of him who raised Jesus from the dead
> dwells in you,
> he who raised Christ from the dead
> will give life to your mortal bodies also
> through his Spirit that dwells in you.
>
> Rom. 8:11

> The Father was wholly in the Son
> when he fulfilled by his incarnation the mystery of
> our salvation.

> Indeed he was not himself incarnate,
> but he was united to the incarnation of the Son.
> And the Spirit was wholly in the Son,
> without indeed being incarnate with him,
> but acting in complete unity with him
> in his incarnation.
>
> St Maximos the Confessor

The Blessed Trinity

It is accepted in Catholic Tradition that all God's activity in his creation, what is called his activity *ad extra*, is a single activity common to Father, Son and Holy Spirit. Where the Father acts, the Son and the Spirit act too; and where the Son acts, the Father and the Spirit also act; and where the Spirit acts, the Father and the Son are also involved in the same action; because all three Persons have the same will and the same action springing from the free decision of that will. It is also clear that, in the case of the Incarnation, and in the whole Christian Mystery, the Persons' relationships to this divine act of salvation differ from one another in a way that reflects the internal relationships they have within the Trinity. If this were not so, then the doctrine of the Blessed Trinity would be reduced to being an interesting fact about God, revealed for its own sake, and with little relevance to salvation beyond the fact that one of the Persons became man.[1] Any exposition of the Christian Mystery must begin and end with the Blessed Trinity because Christian revelation is necessarily Trinitarian in structure. When this is forgotten, Father, Son and Holy Spirit become either different names for the same Reality, or they become three separate people, and each can be invoked without any reference to the other two.

Within the Blessed Trinity, the Father is the Source of the Son and of the Holy Spirit. The Son is eternally generated from the Father by the Holy Spirit; or, the Holy Spirit is the Father's Breath by which the Word is uttered. He is also the love of the Father for the Son and the love of the Son for the Father. St Thomas wrote:

> The Holy Spirit proceeds both from the Father to the Son and from the Son to the Father, not as recipients but as objects of love. For the Holy Spirit is said to proceed from the Father to the Son inasmuch as he is the love whereby the Father loves the Son; and in the same way it may be said that the Holy Spirit proceeds from the Son to the Father inasmuch as he is the love whereby the Son loves the Father. He may be understood, however, to proceed from the Father in as much as the Son receives from the Father the power to spirate the Holy Spirit, and in this sense He cannot be said to proceed from the Son to the Father, seeing that the Father receives nothing from the Son. (QDP 10 4 ad 10)[2]

In other words, the Holy Spirit is the mutual love of Father for the Son and the Son for the Father, and this is the meaning of the famous *filioque* clause in the Creed, 'We believe in the Holy Spirit... who proceeds from the Father and the Son.' But there is a sense in which he proceeds from the Father alone: while the Son can be said to receive the power from the Father to 'breathe' the Holy Spirit, the Father does not receive that power from the Son. The Son is the Image of the Father who is the Source of all that he is, and he does what the Father does; but the Father is not Image of the Son. Instead, through the power of the same Spirit who is in both, the Father is in the Son and the Son is in the Father. St Gregory Palamas, who is an important witness to the Eastern tradition, wrote:

> This Spirit of the Word from on high is like a mysterious love of the Father towards the Word mysteriously begotten; it is the same love as that possessed by the Word and the well-beloved Son of the Father towards him who begat him; this he does insofar as he comes from the Father conjointly with this love, and this love rests naturally on him.[3]

This is echoed by Sergius Bulgakov:

> The Holy Spirit 'proceeds' from the Father to the Son, as the hypostatic love of the Father, which 'abides' in the Son, fulfilling his actuality and possession by the Father. In turn, the Holy Spirit passes 'through' the Son, returning, as it were, to the Father in a mysterious cycle, as the answering hypostatic love of the Son. In this way the Holy Spirit achieves his own fulfilment as the Hypostasis of Love.[4]

The Blessed Trinity in creation

This same Blessed Trinity created the universe to share in the divine life. Fr George Maloney SJ writes:

> If we truly believe that the same Trinity, Father, Son and Holy Spirit, who dwell within us individuals and in the Church, dwell also in their material world as in a temple, then we must be guided by the three-fold presence of the Trinity in the world.
>
> First, from Scripture both in the Old and New Testaments, we believe that the entire created universe comes from God and is being sustained by the actively involved Trinity as creation is being uttered by the Godhead into being by his Word ...
>
> Second, the universe is destined by the Trinity to be guided towards the Trinity as its goal since the whole cosmos is an immense symbol of the Trinity's revelation to us ... We are invited to work in a *synergism*, a working together, to bring all God's creation into full completion through the same Jesus Christ and the Holy Spirit.
>
> Thirdly, more specifically, as we discover the immanent Trinity working within the historical world of the present, we also discern that it has been the same Trinity as working in the historical past up to the present time.[5]

The Father is Creator of the whole cosmos, having formed it with his own 'hands', as St Irenaeus called the Word and the Holy Spirit. However, the universe was not created as a finished product, but as a process which is moving towards a goal; and that goal is Christ. St Maximos the Confessor wrote in the seventh century:

> Christ is the great hidden mystery, the blessed goal, the purpose for which everything was created ... with his gaze fixed on this goal God called things into existence. He [Christ] is the point to which Providence is tending ... He is the mystery which surrounds all ages ... In fact it is for the sake of Christ and for his mystery, that all ages exist and all that they contain. In Christ they have received their principle and their purpose. This synthesis was predetermined at the beginning: a synthesis of the limit and the unlimited, of the measured and the immeasurable, of the bounded and the boundless, of the Creator and the creature, of rest and movement. In the fullness of time the synthesis became visible in Christ, and God's plans were fulfilled.[6]

In our own times, Teilhard de Chardin formed a synthesis between his faith and his scientific knowledge in which the whole universe is evolving towards Christ as *'Omega Point'*. This is very much in accordance with the Greek Fathers, even if his attempt at uniting in a synthesis what he knew as a Christian and what he had come to accept as a scientist is more common in Western Christianity. His starting point is typically Jesuit. As we shall see in chapter 12 on 'The Liturgy of Life', the spiritual writer, Jean-Paul de Caussade begins with the same insight and finds in it the 'sacrament of the present moment' by which we can come into harmony with the divine will. The Jesuit poet, Gerard Manley Hopkins, sees everything 'charged with the glory of God', and recognizes it as the cause of beauty in the universe and hence the inspiration of poetry. The scientist, Teilhard de Chardin, finds in it the motive for scientific activity, so that 'scientific exploration and adoration are activities not so very far apart'. He writes:

> All around us, to right and left, in front and behind, above and below, we have only to go a little beyond the frontier of sensible appearances in order to see the divine welling up and showing through. But it is not only close to us, in front of us, that the divine Presence has revealed itself. It has sprung up so universally, and we find ourselves so surrounded and transfixed by it, that there is no room left to fall down and adore it, even within ourselves.
>
> By means of all created things, without exception, the divine assails us, penetrates us and moulds us. We imagined it as distant and inaccessible, whereas in fact we live steeped in its burning layers. *In eo vivimus.* As Jacob said, awakening from his dream, the world, this palpable world, which we were wont to treat with the boredom and disrespect with which we habitually regard places with no sacred association for us, is in truth a holy place, and we did not know it. *Venite, adoremus.*[7]

This is not a theory for Teilhard de Chardin, but a mystical insight that moves him to intense prayer:

> When your presence, Lord, has flooded me with its light I hoped that within it I might find ultimate reality at its most tangible. But now I have in fact laid hold on you, you who are utter consistency, and I feel myself borne by you, I realize that my deepest hidden desire was not to possess you but to be possessed.
> It is not as a radiation of light, nor as subtilized matter, that I desire you; nor was it thus that I described you in my first intuitive encounter with you; it was as fire. And I can see I shall have no rest unless an active influence, coming forth from you, bears down on me to transform me.
> *The whole universe is aflame.*[8]

Teilhard de Chardin sees the universe as a purposeful process which moves towards the development of consciousness and which becomes more and more intricate in the course of evolution until human intelligence is formed out of the biosphere (the level of living things) and becomes the noosphere, (the level of interacting human intelligence). This human sphere continues to evolve as modern communications bring us together to form an ever more intricate and effective unity. At the same time, because God became man in Palestine two thousand years ago and has given to humanity a share in his life, the noosphere becomes the Christosphere by grace, and Christ will eventually become all in all. Thus nature and the supernatural, creation and salvation, come together in the cosmic Christ who is the meaning of them both. He wrote:

> For christian humanism – faithful in this to the most firmly established theology of the Incarnation – there is no real independence or discordance but a logical subordination between the genesis of humanity in the world and the genesis of Christ, through his Church, in humanity. Inevitably the two processes are structurally linked together, the second needing the first as the material on which it rests in order to supervitalize it. This point of view fully respects the progressive experimental concentration of human thought in a more and more lively awareness of its unifying role; but in place of the undefined point of convergence required as term for this evolution it is the clearly defined personal reality of the incarnate Word that is made manifest to us and established for us as our objective, that Word 'in whom all things subsist'.
> Life for Man: Man for Christ: Christ for God.[9]

We shall see later that the Christian Mystery, like every other reality that is far greater than we are and exists independently of us, can be seen and interpreted from different angles and perspectives without any damage to our understanding and without contradicting each other. For St Maximos the Confessor and the whole tradition that he represents, as well as for Teilhard de Chardin, their centre of interest is the purpose for which God created the universe. This they see as its transformation by sharing in the divine life which became possible through the Incarnation and was realized in Christ by rising from the dead. Thus sin is interpreted, not so much in relationship to the past, as a result of original sin, but in relationship to the future, as a refusal to act in a way consistent with the purpose for which we and the whole universe were made. In the same line of thought, the Holy Spirit continually reveals and brings us into contact with Christ who is the purpose of our existence and in whom the divine purpose of the universe is fulfilled. In the Eucharist, we are brought before the Father by sharing in Christ's death and resurrection, anticipating by grace the fulfilment of this purpose which is the *eschaton*, the New Heaven and the New Earth which shall exist when the present heaven and earth have been transformed into Christ by the presence of the Spirit.

The Holy Spirit and the Incarnation
The Father is the Source and Goal of salvation: 'God was in Christ reconciling the world to himself' (2 Cor. 5:19). The Son alone was incarnate, lived, died on the cross, and rose again. He alone became a part of human history. This leaves us with the Holy Spirit. What is the relationship between the Incarnation and the Spirit? There has to be one because the divine act by which the Son became and remains a human being is as much an act of the Father and the Spirit as it is an act of the Word. That the Spirit was instrumental in bringing about the Incarnation is clear from Luke 1:35. The Spirit was involved in the experience of Jesus at his Baptism where the Father declared him to be his Son (Luke 3:22). This anointing by the Spirit is the reason why Jesus is called *Christ*, and it is

clear that the same Spirit is intimately involved in his public ministry (Luke 4:18) and in his sacrifice (Heb. 9:14) and his resurrection (1 Peter 3:18). Hence, the question: What is the contribution of the Holy Spirit to that act by which God became man and dwelt among us, died for us and rose again? Then there is the further question: In what way does the Spirit continue to operate in the Church and in the world to make salvation effective?

The Incarnation means that Jesus is one divine Person in two natures, the divine and the human. It follows that the divine Person of the Son has two wills, the divine and the human, which are in harmony with each other, and two spheres of operation, acting both as God and Man, with his human activity revealing the action of God-with-us. If Jesus were simply a human individual, cut off from other human beings by time and place, and basically orientated towards his own individual existence and survival in the face of death as distinct from the good of others, his human sphere of operations could not reflect the divine trinitarian activity, and his human personality would not reflect and reveal the divine Person of the Son, who is a Person only because of his relationship with the other Persons of the Trinity. Hence, in order for the Incarnation to happen, it is not enough for the Word to be made flesh, not enough that the human nature of Jesus should exist because of its relationship to God: it is also necessary that the human nature of Jesus should exist because of its radical relationship with the Church, with the whole human race and with the cosmos.

Thus Jesus is not only a historical figure, living at a particular time: he is a human being who, while living at a particular time in history, is a centre of a network of relationships that embrace the whole human race, past, present and future; and these relationships with human persons are a constituent part of Christ's own human personality.[10] In middle-eastern cultures, the king was a kind of collective personality, and people considered what happened to their king as happening to themselves. Both titles, 'Messiah' and 'Son of Man', belong to a particular person who becomes the personification of God's people by fulfilling his God-given role. This is true of Jesus: what happens to him as an individual human being has repercussions in the life of every member of the human race and, indeed, in the history of the whole cosmos; but this is not simply a cultural or political reality as with Eastern potentates: it is a reality belonging to his very being as God incarnate, a dimension of his very humanity made possible by the Spirit. Without this action by the Spirit, the Incarnation could not have taken place because it is this which enables his human nature to be that of the Word who 'enlightens everyone coming into the world' (John 1:9). It was necessary so that, while he remained a historical figure, his human activity could burst the bonds of time and place and embrace the whole of humankind in a love that is both truly divine and truly human. As a consequence, the Blessed Virgin Mary is Mother of all the living (Gen. 3:20) because she is the mother of him who embraces in himself the whole human race. This role requires from her a love for the whole of humankind which she gradually acquired by her intimate relationship with Christ during his life on earth and, most especially, by her participation in his crucifixion (John 10:26).[11]

Without the Spirit, Jesus could not have borne our sins and hence could not have saved us. Because of his Spirit-given solidarity with the whole human race, he suffered the full effects of our separation from his Father: 'My God, my God, why have you abandoned me?' He 'became sin for us', (2 Cor. 5:21), so that his mental suffering on the Cross must have far outstripped his physical pain. However, his obedience unto death, his love that cost him the last drop of his blood, his unswerving fidelity to his Father in spite of everything, reflected the divine love that he has for the Father as a response to the Father's love for him by which he is eternally Son; and his Spirit-given solidarity with the human race ensures that the

Father's love for him spills out on to us, taking the form of pardon for sin, adoption as sons and daughters, and our sanctification by sharing in his divine life. Without Jesus, the Father could not have a proper relationship with human beings; but through Jesus Christ, we become truly his sons, and he becomes our Father.

Without the Spirit Jesus could not have taken on the role of Suffering Servant (Isa. 53) and have borne the sufferings and sins of all humankind because there would have been no real contact between the event of the crucifixion and all those sufferings and sins. In the unity of the Holy Spirit Jesus had a vital contact with all human sufferings and, through his own fidelity unto death, could charge these sufferings with meaning by offering to the sufferers a share in his resurrection. Such is the unity, brought about by the Spirit, between Christ's sufferings and those of the rest of humankind that it can be said either, with Isaiah, that Jesus bore our sufferings or, with Pascal, that Christ is in agony (in all those who suffer) until the end of time. The second-century writer, Melito of Sardis, wrote:

> It is he who endured every kind of suffering in all those who foreshadowed him. In Abel he was slain, in Isaac bound, in Jacob exiled, in Joseph sold, in Moses exposed to die. He was sacrificed in the Passover lamb, persecuted in David, dishonoured in the prophets. It is he who was made man of the Virgin, he who was hung on a tree; it is he who was buried in the earth, raised from the dead, and taken up to the heights of heaven. The type has passed away; the reality has come. The lamb gives place to God; the sheep gives place to a man; and the man is Christ, who fills the whole of creation.[12]

On the same principle, it can be said that Christ suffered in Auschwitz, among the famine-stricken of Africa, the ethnically-cleansed of Bosnia, the bombed-out people of Palestine and Lebanon, and among the victims of suicide bombings in Iraq and Israel; or it can be said that Jesus suffered his Passion two thousand years ago in solidarity with them, the Holy Spirit uniting him to all times and places. All these events added to his pain on the cross; but his fidelity ensured that these happenings, so hopeless in themselves, have become gateways into heaven for those who have even a glimmering of faith, though this faith may be implicit and unformulated, and they do not realize they have it.

The Word became history and lived in a particular time and place, but did so for people of all times and places. His love embraced the whole of human history, from its beginning to the Last Day, and indeed the whole cosmos. His life two thousand years ago and what he did in that space of time, including his death and resurrection, had their effects before he was born, have their effect now, and will continue to affect the human race until the end of the world, because it is the role of the Holy Spirit to ensure that these historic events remain effective for all times, past, present and future, everywhere. Whatever Jesus did for the salvation of humankind remains a historical event; and it is impossible to take it out of its context in time and space and transplant it into another time and space; but, because he offered himself 'through the eternal Spirit', what he did is effective universally. Because he passed from this life to that of the resurrection, the whole universe can look forward to share in the resurrection with him. It follows that, when we celebrate the Eucharist, there are two thousand years between our celebration and the crucifixion; but these two thousand years are no longer an obstacle which separates: the years are bridged by the same Spirit who is not subject to time, who was in Jesus on the cross and is in us and in our Eucharist, so that that the cross and our Eucharist are one single sacrifice, even though neither event is taken out of its historical context.

We too need to learn to love with a truly universal love. Only then will we fulfil our true potential as Catholics (which means *universalists*). What happened to Jesus from the very beginning because it was a necessary dimension of the Incarnation, what happened in Mary through her life with Jesus and her presence at his death, also happens to us by the power of the same Spirit as he transforms us from one degree of glory to another in the image of the Son (2 Cor. 3:18), purifying, deepening and expanding our love until it embraces all creation. *Asceticism* is the stretching, deepening, widening process we have to undergo in collaboration with the Spirit in order that this should happen. Spiritually speaking, we human beings are as small or as large as the things we love. A self-centred person is only as big and as real as the image he has of himself. Growth begins with humility and love. The saints whose love has been transformed by the Holy Spirit have Christ's capacity to love all humankind and the whole cosmos. Thus St Benedict saw everything that exists as a beam of light, which is the love of God. The reason why the Desert Fathers endured the rigours of the desert is because they wished to be so transformed that they would be able to love with this universal love. Only when we love universally does human love and activity reflect the love and activity of God. To transform us by grace so that we love as Christ loves is the work of Christ's Spirit. St Peter Damien says this of a Christian's relationship with the whole Church throughout the world:

> The cohesive force of mutual charity by which the Church is united is so great that she is not merely one in her many members but also, in some mysterious way, present in her entirety in each individual ... By reason of her unity of faith, she has not, in her many members, many parts, and yet through the close-knit bond of charity and the varied charismatic gifts she shows many facets in her individual members. Though the Holy Church is thus diversified in many individuals, she is none the less welded into one by the fire of the Holy Spirit.[13]

St Gregory Palamas explains this in a very realistic fashion. Because we receive Christ in Holy Communion, we are 'bones of his bones and flesh of his flesh'. By carrying him within us we also bear all our brothers because he cannot be separated from his body, the Church. This is also true of our brethren. Hence, when we do good to any one of our brethren, we are also doing good to Christ and to the whole Church because they cannot be separated from Christ and the Church either.[14] We also see him in our brothers.

Because of the Spirit, the human life and the Passion of Jesus Christ are a living reality to us, even if they did happen two thousand years ago. They have brought about change before they happened, while they were happening, and are changing things now, long after they happened. Christ's Passion and death gave value and meaning to a long string of events in Old Testament times, culminating in the Immaculate Conception of the Blessed Virgin who was conceived without sin because of the foreseen merits of her Son. All this was Old Testament grace, given by God to prepare for the coming of Jesus; but it was a grace that already reflected the face of him who was to come, an effect before it happened of Christ's death on the cross. At the Annunciation, the Holy Spirit brought about the Incarnation in the womb of the Blessed Virgin, thus initiating a new kind of relationship between God and human beings based on the union of the divine and human natures in Christ, firstly in Mary and then, through the death and resurrection of Christ, with the Church; and, at the end of time, the whole of creation will be transformed by it. It was at Pentecost that the risen Christ began a new kind of presence among us through the infusion of the Spirit in the Church, thus anticipating the End Time when God will be all in all.

The unity of the Church
Christ is present in the Church as a whole, in each Christian community and in each Christian person through the

power of the Spirit. The same Spirit is Source both of the diversity of functions within the Church and of their unity in Christ which make them functions of Christ's body (1 Cor. 12:4ff). Through the Spirit Christians are given understanding of the things of God because they share the mind of Christ (1 Cor. 2:11 ff). The Holy Spirit is also actively involved in the growth in holiness of each individual Christian as he forms him little by little into the image of Christ (2 Cor. 3:17–18). Thus the Spirit forges our unity in Christ through the formation and animation of church structures, by giving us a common understanding of Christ's revelation, and by fostering our interior holiness. When we pray in the Eucharist to the Father to send his Spirit on the Church to make it one in a prayer that is called the *epiclesis* (see ch. 4), we are asking for him to act at all these three levels because Christian unity involves everything from a universally-recognized ministry working for the common good to purity of heart in the individual.

The memory of the Church

The Holy Spirit is the living *memory* of the Church, bringing alive and making effective in the present the wonderful deeds of God from the past, and even of the future, not by abolishing time or travelling through time, but by bridging it with his eternal action. Let us quote Rowan Williams again:

> [Moses and Elijah] lived hundreds of years before him, yet what makes them radiant, what makes them agents of God, is the light coming from Jesus, so this icon – like the story it illustrates – confuses our ordinary sense of time ... In Jesus, the world of ordinary prosaic time is not destroyed, but it is broken up and reconnected, it works no longer just in straight lines, but in layers and spirals of meaning.[15]

God's relationship with time is fundamentally different

from ours: he has the same living contact with past and future as he has with the present. When we are brought by the Holy Spirit into a relationship with the Father through Christ, we come to share in his living contact with the life, death and resurrection of Christ. Hence, when we ask the Father in the Eucharist to 'remember' these events in the past, and the Second Coming in the future, God sees them as living events in the same way as he sees our celebration, and we are brought into a relationship with these events as we share in their saving effect, we 'die and rise' with Christ. In the Christian dispensation, the Church on earth is one with the Church in heaven, time and eternity meet, and the Holy Spirit makes effective for us in the present all that God has done for us in the past, and anticipates in us that relationship between God and his creation which belongs to the end time when there will be a new heaven and a new earth. Hence the Church's memory is a participation in the 'memory' of God in Christ through the ministry of the Spirit. It is within the context of this memory that the Scriptures were written; and it is according to this memory, experienced in and by the Church, especially in the Eucharist, that the Scriptures are understood. This relationship between time and eternity is illustrated in the religious icons of the East, as explained by Dr Williams. We call this Christian memory that brings us into contact with what is remembered by its Greek name, '*anamnesis*'.

The Eucharistic Prayer is *anamnesis*, a bringing to mind; but it is also an *epiclesis*, an invocation, asking the Father to send his Spirit on the bread and wine and on us so that our *memorial* in the Presence of the Father may become effective. By so doing, we become one with Christ in his self-offering and share in his resurrected life. In Western tradition, the consecration of the bread and wine is seen to take place at the point when the Last Supper is remembered, because this memory before God and the Church is made alive and effective by the Spirit. In Eastern tradition, the consecration is seen to take place at the invocation for the Holy Spirit because God has guaranteed that a petition for the Holy Spirit will always be granted by the Father and because it is the Holy Spirit that makes the words of Christ effective. Liturgists from both traditions accept that the consecration prayer is the Eucharistic prayer as a whole, and that it is, by its very nature, an *anamnesis* and an *epiclesis*. The exact moment when the great change occurs is secondary and can vary from rite to rite.

Communion across time and space

The sacraments are acts of Christ in the power of the Spirit. Just as the death and resurrection of Christ played an effective role in the times preparatory to his coming, were made cosmic events at the time of their happening, and continue to be effective for salvation until the end of time, so, by the power of the same Spirit, the effects of the sacraments can be seen even in the time preparatory to their celebration, and they can continue to be effective long after the celebration is over. By the same token, they are acts of the whole Church and not just acts of the local congregation. The presence of the Holy Spirit ensures that the local church is the manifestation in one place of the whole Church, past, present and future; it is the present manifestation of the Church in every place, which is the Church of heaven and of earth. It is also due to the Spirit's presence that the whole Church on earth has a true understanding of God's revelation, so that it can offer true worship to God in every place on behalf of all humankind.

By means of the Spirit, the Church transcends nationality

Pope Benedict XVI sees the papacy as an institution radically opposed to the identification of the Church with any nation. No one calls Italy 'holy Italy' because the papacy is there. In countries like Poland, the complete identification of the Polish Catholic Church with the Polish nation is avoided by the allegiance of the Poles to the Roman See. In the Pope's youth, the Nazis favoured a form of Christianity which supported and blessed the *volk*, the German nation. He noticed how too close an identification of the Church with the nation in history was a major factor in bringing about schism, in making hatred between Christians acceptable, in fomenting discord in the very Church that was founded to be an icon of God's peace. Thus, what is now called the Assyrian Church of the East was not invited to Ephesus, because it was outside the Roman Empire, but it was then expected to adopt the formulations of Ephesus, imposed from the outside by officials of an empire it rejected. The enmity between the Church in Egypt and Ethiopia towards the Empire was a factor in their refusing to accept Chalcedon, and supporters of Chalcedon in Syria and Egypt are called *Melkites* (king's men). It is clear that the identification of the Eastern Orthodox Church with the Eastern Empire and the Western Latin Church with the Western Empire led to Rome being accused of putting the *filioque* in the Creed long before it actually did so, and helped to estrange the two sides. Moreover, the Catholic Church's too-close identification with civil authorities led its authorities to hand heretics over to be burned. Ratzinger saw how one of the main reasons why Protestantism became established in Germany and England was because of the desire to identify the Church with the nation. He saw the terrible example of ethnic cleansing in Greece and Turkey which led to suffering on both sides, and, in Turkey, the elimination of churches which had thrived since apostolic times. Closer to our time, he saw that the ethnic cleansing of Serbia, blessed by bishops, led to the cold-blooded murder of men, women and children, and the equally terrible backlash by nationalistic Catholics. He believes that mixing together the aspirations of religion and nationality can lead to a diabolical distortion of both.

The Eucharist shows us that nationality is transcended in our Christian life. We have seen that the Church is fully itself when it celebrates the Eucharist. In the Eucharist the local congregation is only the tip of the iceberg. The Holy Spirit unites in each celebration all the angels and saints, all who celebrate the Eucharist throughout history and in every place, all who are baptized of every nation, whether rich or poor. With all of them we are one single body. Moreover, through this act of Christ's body, grace pours out on all humankind according to the receptivity of each person. Nationality has nothing to do with the process. As St Irenaeus wrote, 'Our thinking is in accordance with the Eucharist, and the Eucharist confirms our thinking.'

As a young theologian, Fr Joseph Ratzinger noted that the pagan Romans had accused the Christians of being a people without a homeland. The pagans believed that religion is an aspect of nationhood, and loyalty to the gods was an aspect of loyalty to the established order. In contrast, Diognetus said of Christians that they were at home everywhere but belonged to no place on earth. A pagan called Celsus brought this as an accusation to Origen; and Origen accepted that Christianity had severed the connection between religion and nationality. Indeed, Christ liberated people from allegiance to the evil angels that govern each nation, and has brought them under Christ into the unity of the Church. He wrote:

> Whoever delivers himself over to what is national, and, in place of thinking and living humanly, thinks and lives in the confines of a nation, such a one places himself under the sway of his evil angel.[16]

In another place, Origen does give the nations a preparatory role in relation to the Gospel; but it is clear that for him they are an aspect of the world that is passing away and have no part in the world of the resurrection. The Fathers taught that the Word, in assuming human nature, took to himself what every human being has in common with all others. Here again, nationality is irrelevant.

Finally, Fr Ratzinger was convinced that the classical work of St Augustine, *De Civitate Dei*, is an attack on political religion. To attain the peoples' allegiance, the state offers false values and unreal gods; and behind these are the very real powers of the devil and his angels: we have to choose either the city of fallen men which Scripture calls the Tower of Babel, with humanity divided by different kinds of egotism, or the City of God with its allegiance to God the Creator of the universe, and with its love for the whole of humankind and of every single human being, a reflection of God's love for humanity manifested in the Incarnation.

Ratzinger has been, and probably still is, very concerned that the Church's openness to the world should not cause it to become worldly. There is an authentic openness to the world that springs from the fact that the Holy Trinity has opened itself to creation through the Incarnation; and there is a false openness which involves adopting the world's values, nationalism being one value that should be left outside the church doors. He wrote:

> There is only one legitimate form of the Church's openness to the world, and so must it always certainly be. That form is two-fold. It is: mission as a prolongation of the movement of the Word's procession, and the simple gesture of disinterested serving love in the actualising of the divine love, a love which streams forth even when it remains without response.

Hence the Church should not be so organized as to foment any form of nationalism that impedes the flow of disinterested, serving love between its members after the manner of the Blessed Trinity, nor that obscures its witness to the rest of humankind to the kind of unity across borders that God wishes for humanity. The papacy ensures as far as it is possible that no local or regional institution so closes in on itself in a way as to stop the flow of love across frontiers between its members. For this reason, all authority within the Church, local, national and regional, is subject to papal authority. His ideal of unity is beautifully expressed in the new Eucharistic Prayer V(d) in use in the Latin Rite. After praying for the Holy Spirit to come down on the people, it goes on:

> Grant that our church of (N) be constantly renewed in the light of the Gospel and may always find new impulses of life; strengthen the ties of unity between the laity and the pastors of your Church, between our bishop (N) and his priests and deacons, between all the bishops and Pope (Benedict); that the Church may become, in the middle of our world divided by war and discord, an instrument of unity, of concord and of peace.

Of course, many nations and cultures have a long history of openness to the Holy Spirit, and this has left them a legacy of customs, rites, music and other arts of which they are justly proud and which continues to nurture their spirit. Once patriotism as a xenophobic turning-in on oneself has been decisively renounced in favour of universal love, these differences between nations and cultures can only enrich the whole Church and the whole of humankind. The Roman See is under a moral obligation to respect these differences, just as it has to respect all the works of the Spirit in the Church.

The presence of the kingdom

Our faith transcends nationality because, in the Eucharist, we are raised up to become members of the kingdom. The Holy Spirit is the presence of the kingdom of God which was planted through Christ's loving obedience unto death in his resurrected human nature, a foretaste of which is found in the Christian life in general and in the Eucharist in particular; and this Spirit will one day transform the whole universe into Christ, when God will be all in all. Just as the Spirit is the bridge between Christ's life, death and resurrection and all times and

The Role of the Spirit in the Christian Mystery 39

places, he is also the bridge between the present and the future, between us and the Last Day; and he is the bridge between us and the presence of the Father in heaven who will transform the cosmos into a new heaven and earth. By our baptism we are already citizens of this kingdom; and, to the extent that we leave behind worldly ways and become one with the risen Christ, to that extent we will be his witnesses before the world.

Notes

1. See the very cogent argument by Karl Rahner SJ in his book *The Trinity* (Herder & Herder, 1970), ch.1.
2. Quoted from Michael D. Torre, 'St John Damascene and St Thomas Aquinas on the Eternal Procession of the Holy Spirit' in *St Vladimir's Theological Quarterly*, 1994, 8:3, pp. 303–7.
3. Quoted from the same excellent article by Torre, above. Taken from St Gregory Palamas, *Physical Chapters PG* 150 col. 1144D–1145A. Complete translation in *St Vladimir's Theological Quarterly*, 1972, 16:2, pp. 83–9.
4. cf. Serge Bulgakov, *The Comforter* (Eerdmans, Grand Rapids, 2004), p. 181.
5. George Maloney SJ, *God's Community of Love* (New City Press, 1993).
6. *Questions to Thalassios*, 60 (*PG* 90.612). Olivier Clément, *The Roots of Christian Mysticism* (New City, 1993), p. 39.
7. Pierre Teilhard de Chardin, *The Divine Milieu* (Collins, 1960), p. 99.
8. Pierre Teilhard de Chardin, *The Hymn of the Universe* (Fontana, Collins, 1970), p. 72.
9. Ibid., p. 79.
10. John Zizioulas, *Being as Communion* (St Vladimir's Seminary Press, New York, 1985), pp. 123–32. A wonderful book, if read critically. Zizioulas is a giant among theologians.
11. See the Epilogue, below.
12. See above, ch. 1, n. 2.
13. St Peter Damien in *The Dominus Vobiscum*, chs. 5, 6 and 10. (*PL* cxlv, 235–6), taken from Henri de Lubac, *Catholicism* (Burns & Oates, 1962), p. 273.
14. John Meyendorff, *A Study of Gregory Palamas* (Faith Press, 1964), p. 179.
15. Rowan Williams, *The Dwelling of the Light* (Canterbury Press, Norwich, 2003), p. 7f.
16. *Contra Celsum* V.32. Quoted from Aidan Nichols OP, *The Theology of Joseph Ratzinger* (T&T Clark, 1988). I owe much to this book for this section.

Chapter Three

More Ways than One

Within Catholicism, the unity of the Christian Mystery allowed people at different times and in different places to focus on one particular doctrine and to make it the key for their understanding of the whole. We see the classic pattern in the Liturgy. Here the climax of everything is the resurrection of Christ. If Christ had not risen, then our faith would be in vain. If we die with Christ, it is in order to live with him. In the Eucharist we celebrate with the risen Christ the memorial of his death. 'Christ is risen!' 'He has risen indeed!' The icon portrays the Gospel in a world transformed by the light of Tabor and of the resurrection. However, all other feasts and seasons lead us to appreciate different aspects of the same Mystery, as does the best of Western Christian art. For instance, there are liturgical texts and references which belong to the primitive Church in which the Baptism of Jesus and his death and resurrection are so connected that themes which normally belong to the interpretation of his death, such as his defeat of the devil and cosmic victory, were associated with the Baptism, while in St Mark's Gospel, Jesus refers to his suffering and death as his baptism. In the Middle Ages there was a new emphasis on the humanity of Christ, especially his humble birth and his passion and death on the cross. The Christmas crib, and statues and paintings of Jesus as a baby and of Jesus suffering, became commonplace, and imitating

Jesus in his life and in his sufferings became an ideal.

Meister Eckhart put his emphasis on the birth of Christ. He said that Jesus was born in Bethlehem so that he could be born in the soul of each one of us. By this he meant a presence and activity of Christ in the soul that is richer and on a different plane from that of his presence to keep us in existence, which is only a preparation for his presence by grace. Charles de Foucauld's gateway into the Christian Mystery was Nazareth: the thirty years Jesus spent unknown and anonymous as the son of a carpenter, in humble obedience to his divine Father. Charles de Foucauld's ambition was to live among people in the same way and become a vehicle of Christ's presence. Of course, he knew that this is possible only because Jesus died and rose again, and he wanted to share in the humiliation and rejection that Christ suffered on the cross, even while living humbly among the poorest of the poor in his 'Nazareth'.

In a place called San Miguel, high in the Peruvian Andes, the people come up to kiss the cross on Good Friday. It is not the glorious cross of Christ's victory in the spirit of the liturgy, but they kiss the feet of the dead Christ, wounded and bleeding for our sins. Latin American crucifixes vie with one another in depicting blood and death. 'Where is the resurrection?' you may well ask, especially if the crucifix emphasizes Christ's suffering with gory detail. Actually, the resurrection is usually implied in the title of the crucifix: titles like 'Lord of the Miracles', 'Lord of the Agony' etc. remind us that he who died has risen, conquering pain and death, so that, while the people concentrate on Christ's death, they do so with confidence. There is one crucifix in my area of Peru called the 'Christ of Life'. The risen Christ is a mystery, beyond human ken, but we can imagine Christ dying for us. Moreover, injustice and death are commonplace in Latin America, and many can identify themselves with Christ's suffering because suffering is a part of their daily experience. At the same time, by looking at the image of the dead Christ, they gain some insight into how much the risen Christ loves them.

If you were to put the cross of Christ two thousand years in the past, while making the resurrection contemporary with us, this would falsify your understanding of both the cross and the resurrection. Look at the picture of the 'Lord of the Miracles' in Lima, a dead Christ with Our Lady and Mary Magdalene weeping at his feet, and then see the heroic-looking Anglo-Saxon he-man, often used to represent the risen Christ in modern repository art; and then ask yourself which is a more faithful depiction of the resurrection. The handsome, broad-shouldered, blue-eyed Christ tells us something about our idea of what a conquering hero should look like on television, but nothing about Christ. The 'Lord of the Miracles' tells us that the resurrection is crucified love transformed. The proof of this love is that he loved his people to the last drop of his blood; and it continues to be effective on their behalf because he has risen from the dead. Without his resurrection, Christ's death would not make sense and our faith would be in vain. Without his death, Christ's resurrection would be an interesting fact but completely irrelevant to our salvation. In Christ, death and resurrection belong to each other. Peruvian peasants know this by instinct. The essential unity between the passion and the resurrection was actually lived by St Paul who said,

> I have been crucified with Christ; it is no longer I who live but Christ who lives in me, and the life I now live in the flesh I live by faith in the Son of God who loved me and gave himself for me. (Gal. 2:20)

Edith Stein (St Teresa Benedicta of the Cross) comments:

> Faith in the Crucified – a living faith joined to loving surrender – is for us entrance into life and the beginning of future glory. The cross, therefore, is our only claim to glory. 'Far be it from me to glory except in the

cross of Our Lord Jesus Christ, by which the world has been crucified to me, and I to the world.' He who has decided for Christ is dead to the world and the world to him. He carries in his body the marks of the Lord's wounds, is weak and despised by the people but is precisely therefore strong because the power of God is mighty in the weak.[1]

Julian of Norwich also sees the contemplation of the cross as the gateway to heaven; and St John of the Cross would go into ecstasy whenever he saw a crucifix. In the Christian religion, life comes out of death, and joy out of self-denial.

These changes of focus from Christ's resurrection to his incarnation or to his life in Nazareth or to his passion are only possible because of the organic unity of all the different doctrines in the one Christian Mystery. They are all windows through which we can look at the whole Mystery. Even the divine motherhood of Mary has been used by saints as their entrance into the complete Christian revelation.

In the Gospels, characteristics and themes that one would have thought belong to Christ only after his resurrection keep on making their appearance in accounts of what happened beforehand. For instance, St Luke celebrates the whole doctrine of our redemption as well as Christian discipleship in his account of the annunciation and the birth of Jesus. In the Gospel of St John it looks as though the characteristics of the risen Lord are read back into stories of his earthly life. As the Word made flesh, those who saw him saw the Father; and he was the heavenly temple where the Father dwelt, of which the temple in Jerusalem was only a copy, so that blood and water flowed from his side after his sacrifice, as it did from the temple whenever they washed the altar after the sacrifices were over. For St John, God appears to us in his glory in Christ's death, and according to its attitude to Christ on the cross the whole world is judged – a theme normally associated with the end of time. Because each incident in the Jesus story is a moment in and a revelation of the single redemptive act of God, the authors of the Gospels saw the whole story reflected in each incident, salvation in the healing of the blind and the deaf, the cosmic war between God and the devil in the casting out of demons, the resurrection in the raising of Lazarus, and the last judgement in the cross. The sacraments, and especially the Eucharist and Baptism, are also windows into the whole Christian Mystery because, as St Leo the Great said, what was visible in Christ during his life on earth has passed over into the sacraments. Thus from one point of view we can say with Mark the Hermit that the whole Christian life is an unfolding of baptismal grace; and from another, we can say that baptism is an entry into the Eucharistic Assembly where the whole Christian Mystery is present.

Vladimir Lossky, in his book, *The Mystical Theology of the Eastern Church*, points out the differences between Orthodox saints and Catholic ones. He writes:

> The cult of the humanity of Christ is foreign to Eastern tradition; or, rather, this deified humanity always assumes for the Orthodox Christian that same glorious form under which it appeared to the disciples on Mount Tabor: the humanity of the Son, manifesting forth that deity which is common to the Father and the Spirit. The way of the imitation of Christ is never practised in the spiritual life of the Eastern Church. Indeed, for the Orthodox Christian this way seems to have a certain lack of fullness: it would seem to imply an attitude somewhat external in regard to Christ. For Eastern spirituality the only way which makes us conformable to Christ is that of the acquisition of the grace which the Holy Spirit confers. No saint of the Eastern Church has ever borne the stigmata, those outward marks which have made certain great Western saints and mystics as it were living patterns of the

suffering Christ. But, by contrast, Eastern saints have very frequently been transfigured by the inward light of uncreated grace, and have appeared resplendent, like Christ on the mount of Transfiguration.[2]

There is a sectarian attitude among some Orthodox theologians who oppose theological positions and spiritualities which, in fact, are complementary. Indeed, this attitude has been present on both sides of the divide, but it has lasted longer among the Orthodox. This is certainly the case here. While the Eastern Orthodox see the life and death of Jesus through the glow of his resurrection, the Franciscan school of spirituality – I have never heard of a Benedictine mystic receiving the stigmata – glimpses the resurrection through the sufferings of the Passion. The problem is that, learned as Vladimir Lossky is in the ways of the West, he sees it all from outside. Let us look at two saints, one Russian Orthodox, St Seraphim of Sarov, and the other an Italian Catholic, Padre Pio. Both had an intense love of Christ and a great compassion for those in need. Both, after much suffering, had many charismatic gifts, insight into souls, prophecy, healing and so on. Both were visited from a very young age by Our Lady and the same saints, who showed a wanton disregard for theological niceties, ecclesiastical divisions and historical antagonisms. Both were known to give out an intense scent of flowers. Most of all, both participated as priests in the Liturgy in which Christ manifested his presence to them in Word and Sacrament, and the Holy Spirit transformed the bread and wine into the body and blood of Christ, confirmed their faith in truth, as St Irenaeus wrote; and formed Padre Pio and St Seraphim, with their different spiritualities, into the image of Christ.

Padre Pio as a young man was very preoccupied with the sufferings of the poor and asked God what he could do. He was asked to take on some of the sufferings himself. The Eastern saint, St Isaac of Nineveh, when he speaks of a compassionate heart, could be describing

Padre Pio: 'His heart breaks when he sees the pain and the suffering of the humblest creatures.' Padre Pio was further asked to share in the sufferings of Christ for the world. This he did with the stigmata and with times of desolation of soul. However, it was not, as Lossky suggested, implying an 'attitude somewhat external with regard to Christ'. It manifested solidarity with the love of Christ, fruit of the Holy Spirit's presence in the depths of Padre Pio's soul.

St Seraphim was a monk who, after many years in his community, was given permission to live as a solitary in the Russian forest. His reputation for sanctity grew, and he became a *staretz*, a kind of spiritual father, and people came from far and near to seek advice and to receive God's blessing. Like St Martin de Porres who showed an equal richness in charismatic gifts in seventeenth-century Lima, St Seraphim encountered opposition in his own community — human nature being the same everywhere — and the abbot ordered him not to receive people in his forest cell. He obeyed, and there followed a thousand days of solitude, which he spent, for the most part, praying on a rock and being attacked by the devil. A new abbot, who had been elected from among those who opposed the whole institution of the *staretz*, ordered him back to the monastery. He returned but remained incommunicado for some time, continuing his life of solitary prayer. Then, one day, for no discernible reason, he opened his door and began to accept those who came to him. His greeting, 'Christ has risen!' by itself cured sicknesses, resolved problems, and led penitents to God. People from all walks of life, from members of the imperial family to peasants, but especially children, came to share in his closeness to God — the same reason why crowds travelled to see Padre Pio — and he served them without restriction to the end of his days.

It is not as though the two spiritualities are mutually exclusive. Padre Pio suffered dreadful desolation of soul which he bore patiently in solidarity with Christ and the poor; but he also went frequently into ecstasy, quite often for several hours at a time; and I don't suppose St Seraphim was all that happy while praying for a thousand days on the rock. Moreover, although St Francis of Assisi had the stigmata, he was no stranger to the light of Tabor, although he probably did not describe it in that way, having a different spirituality and theological language. On one occasion, he and his brothers had a meeting with St Clare and some of her sisters in a house. Before settling down to eat, the Lord swept into their prayer, and the whole company was lost in contemplation. So much light was generated on that occasion that the neighbours thought the house was on fire.[3]

As a monk with 'charismatic' leanings, I am more drawn to the spirituality of St Seraphim than that of Padre Pio, and I have an icon of him in my monastic cell; but, because of the organic unity of the Christian Mystery, I can choose any road to sanctity which is consistent with it. One of the many evils of schism is that it becomes possible to pit two forms of genuine sanctity against one another, which is an offence against charity. I hope that, one day, both Catholics and Orthodox will recognize the truth in each other, re-discover their unity, and feel free to savour the liberty that will enable them to choose, without any feeling of disloyalty to their own tradition. I do not believe that St Seraphim is, in some way, better or worse than Padre Pio. I am sure that, in spite of the theologians, in spite of their different traditions, or rather, because they *lived* them so generously, both are now in harmony with God in heaven, and both will pray for us as I and my readers limp along the road to eventual sanctity, participating in the many-faceted but unique Mystery of Christ.

Notes

1. All my quotations from Edith Stein have been taken from two excellent books which, unfortunately, I do not have with me in Peru. They are: *Edith Stein: A Personal Portrait* by Pat Lyne, and *Edith Stein: Woman of Prayer* by Joanne Moseley. Both are short,

clear and informative, and they complement one another. Both are published by Gracewing.
2. V. Lossky, *The Mystical Theology of the Eastern Church* (James Clarke & Co. Ltd, Cambridge, 1957), p. 243.
3. See ch. 5 below.

Chapter Four

God is with us in Christ

According to the Constitution on the Liturgy *Sacrosanctum Concilium*, the chief characteristic of liturgy in general and of the Mass in particular is the presence and participation of Christ from beginning to end. It states:

> The liturgy is considered as an exercise of the priestly office of Jesus Christ. In the liturgy the sanctification of man is manifested by signs perceptible to the senses, and is effected in a way that is proper to each of these signs; in the liturgy full public worship is performed by the Mystical Body of Jesus Christ, that is, by the Head and His members. (*SC* 1. 7)[1]

Because Christ sits at the right hand of the Father as well as being present in the Church community, in the earthly liturgy we share in the heavenly liturgy:

> In the earthly liturgy, by way of foretaste, we share in that heavenly liturgy which is celebrated in the holy city of Jerusalem toward which we journey as pilgrims, and in which Christ is sitting at the right hand of God, a minister of the sanctuary and of the true tabernacle. (*SC* 1. 8)[2]

This reflects the insight of the Letter to the Hebrews. Christ is present in his body the Church, but, at the same time, he is at home in the presence of the Father, and we are with him:

> You have come to Mount Zion and to the city of the living God, the heavenly Jerusalem, and to innumerable angels in festal gathering, and to the assembly of the firstborn who are enrolled in heaven, and to God the judge of all, and to the spirits of the righteous made perfect, and to Jesus, the mediator of a new covenant, and to the sprinkled blood that speaks a better word than the blood of Abel ... Therefore, since we are receiving a kingdom that cannot be shaken, let us give thanks, by which we offer to God an acceptable worship with *reverence* and *awe*, for indeed our God is a consuming fire. (Heb. 12:22-9)

In the Mass, Christ is not absent until the consecration: he is present right from the very beginning and *manifests* this presence in various ways, because the Mass is the prayer and celebration of the whole body, head and members, Christ and the Christian community; and what the community does in his name, Christ does through it. He is present in all parts of the liturgy, praying, proclaiming through his body, the Church, but in the specifically Eucharistic part he offers himself to us as food and drink, and in doing so, offers himself to his Father as our representative. This is the same act of self-offering in which, by putting himself into the hands of men, he suffered death and thus merited for himself and for us the life of the resurrection. Christ is the main actor and the priest a mere instrument. It is not necessary for the priest to be prominent: it is necessary for Christ to be prominent. The constitution tells us:

> Christ is always present in His Church, especially in her liturgical celebrations. He is present in the sacrifice of the Mass, not only in the person of His minister, 'the same one now offering, through the ministry of priests,

who formerly offered himself on the cross,' but especially under the Eucharistic species. By His power He is present in his sacraments, so that when a man baptizes it is really Christ Himself who baptizes. He is present in His word, since it is He Himself who speaks when the holy Scriptures are read in the church. He is present, finally, when the Church prays and sings, for He promised: 'Where two or three are gathered together for my sake, there I am in the midst of them.' (Matt. 18:20)[3]

We could use any of the Eucharistic prayers in the new rite to illustrate the activity of Christ in the Mass; but we shall use Eucharistic Prayer III. Just as the Mass begins with 'In the Name of the Father and of the Son and of the Holy Spirit', and ends with the Trinitarian blessing, so the Eucharistic prayer begins with two mentions of the holy Trinity and ends with the doxology. This is what scholars call an *inclusion*, and it means that the whole prayer and even the whole celebration are filled with the activity of the Blessed Trinity.

The prayer opens with the statement that connects the Mass with everything else: everything that exists rightly praises the Father because all life, all holiness comes from Him through Jesus Christ by the work of the Holy Spirit. The Father is the Source of both the Son and the Holy Spirit, and is the Source of all blessings in his creation. He generates the Son by the breath of the Holy Spirit, so that Father and Son are one in the same Spirit. In St Luke's Gospel, the Father sends his Spirit who overshadows the Blessed Virgin and thus brings about the Incarnation. Many years later, after Christ's baptism in the Jordan by John, the Spirit descends on Jesus who hears a voice from heaven saying, 'You are my Son, the beloved, with you I am well pleased' (Luke 3:21–2). The descent of the Holy Spirit from the Father was a permanent characteristic, for which reason Jesus was called the *Christ*, or the *Anointed One*. However, the same Spirit was the link by which he offered himself to the Father: as it says in the Letter to the Hebrews, '... how much more will the blood of Christ who through the *eternal Spirit* offered himself without blemish to God, purify our consciences from dead works to worship the living God' (Heb. 9:14). Thus the Holy Spirit is the Gift of Love of the Father to the Son and of the Son to the Father; and his purifying action in us is linked with worship.

The Father in this Eucharistic Prayer is portrayed as the Source of all life and holiness, through the Son, in the Holy Spirit; and he is the Goal to which we all are moving, as the Holy Spirit scoops us up in the doxology and brings us through the Son into the Father's Presence. We thus participate in this flow of love between Father and Son, sharing in their communion by sharing in the Spirit. Another name for all this is 'salvation'; and this is what we are so thankfully celebrating in the Mass.

In Jewish tradition, everything that is created praises God simply by existing: but angels and human beings have the intelligence to recognize God in his works, and thus the vocation to praise God on behalf of creation. In this movement towards God, human beings have a special place because we combine within ourselves both the spiritual and the material worlds. We were also to be the instrument by which God's love would bring the world to perfection through us. All this changed with our sin and the loss of *synergy*[4] between our wills and the will of God.

The prayer then goes from the general to the particular. God gathers a people to himself *so that*, from the rising of the sun to its setting, a perfect sacrifice may be made. It is only because of this Trinitarian activity of gathering us together that we are enabled to approach the Father in praise, together with Christ, in the unity of the Holy Spirit. The offering of the Eucharist is thus the Church's main function: at least this is true as long as it is remembered that there is much more to celebrating the Eucharist than taking part in a ceremony: we are only truly participating in the Mass if we are living Eucharistic lives. Every aspect and circumstance of our lives and every human relationship, in so far as they are Christian, are taken up and offered to God because they are transformed into Christ's offering. However, we offer this sacrifice, not only for our own salvation, but on behalf of everything that exists, and we present all authentically human activities of the whole human race to be transformed into the same sacrifice of Christ, thus giving to the world of human beings a dimension that it would not have without us. In Christ we are the voice of the human race speaking to God, offering true worship on behalf of all, being receptive to God's grace on behalf of all; and we are the voice of material creation, of the whole cosmos, responding to God's creative love, a vocation that Adam rejected when he sinned, but which was restored to us by Christ, firstly in himself as man, and secondly in us, as we enter the Christian Mystery.

By this two-way ministry of the Spirit, Jesus is exercising his priestly function: he is the *human face* of God in God's dealings with us, and the *acceptable face* of humankind and of all creation as he represents us to the Father from within the depths of the Trinity. Through the Incarnation, his self-offering as man becomes the vehicle of the Holy Spirit whom the Father gives to the Son to be the two-way flow of life between them. The Father gives all that he is to the Son, thus constituting him as Son, and receives the self-offering of the Son as he surrenders all he is to the Father, acknowledging the Father to be the Source of his very being. Now the love by which the Father and the Son give and receive from each other is the Holy Spirit; and it is the Holy Spirit who binds us to Christ in the Mass so that, together with Christ, we too can give our 'all' to the Father and, together with Christ, receive the Father's 'all', his own divine life, becoming sons in the Son. Christ receives this life because it is his nature to receive it, and we receive it as a gift or *grace*, but it is the same life, and we become truly sons and daughters of God the Father. This process was called by the Fathers *theosis* or divinization. Of this Nicholas Cabasilas wrote:

> Men (inserted into Christ) are converted into gods and sons of God ... Dust is raised to a level of glory which practically equal in honour and divinity to the divine nature.
> Why do we speak of adoptive sonship when this divine sonship goes more deep that natural sonship, and those who receive this birth are more sons (of God) than they are sons of their parents? There is a greater difference between divine sonship and natural, than there is between natural sonship and adoptive. What makes the relationship between father and son real? The simple fact that our flesh comes from his flesh and our life is supported by the blood we get from him. The same is brought about by our Saviour: we are flesh of his flesh and bones of his bones.[5]

The priest continues with the epiclesis, a prayer to the Father to send his Spirit on the bread and wine and on the Church. In Genesis 1:2 the Spirit of God hovers over the primeval soup, drawing out order from chaos and executing the commands of God's Word, thus creating the universe. In the Mass, the same Spirit hovers over the bread and wine and, at the Father's Word, transforms it into the New Creation, which is really the old creation shot through and through with the divine Life. In God's good time, it will be a 'new heaven and a new earth', but, at present, it is all concentrated in the risen Christ, and the place to find him is the Mass. Narsai of Nisibis (399–502) wrote:

> The priest invites the Spirit to descend and to hover over the bread and wine, making them the body and blood of Christ the king. He also asks that the Spirit hover over the assembly, to make it worthy to receive the body and blood of Christ. The priest makes this

supplication with intense feeling, drawing himself up and raising his hands to heaven. The priest looks up to heaven with confidence and begs the Holy Spirit to come to complete the mysteries which he has offered. The Holy Spirit descends at the request of the priest who celebrates the mysteries, (whatever his sins may be), because the priest is mediator. The priest invites the Holy Spirit to descend on the offering, and he prostrates himself with fear and trembling, filled with awe.[6]

Then the priest recites or sings the words of institution; and, as he remembers with us the Last Supper and what Jesus did there in the presence of the Father, the Holy Spirit makes efficacious the words of Christ in the present. St John Chrysostom wrote:

> The priest says, 'This is my body', and these words change the nature of the offerings. Thus the word of the Saviour, pronounced once, has sufficed and will suffice to fulfil the most perfect sacrifice on the altar of every church, from the Last Supper of Jesus Christ right up to our time and till his coming again.
> The bread becomes the bread of heaven, because the Spirit comes to rest upon it. What is there in front of us is not the work of any human power. He who did this at the Last Supper still does it now. For our part, we hold the rank of servants: it is he who sanctifies and transforms.
> There is only one Christ, whole and entire now as then, a single body ... We do not offer another victim as the high priest of those days did [in the Old Testament]. It is always the same victim, or rather we make a memorial of the sacrifice.[7]

The priest continues to present before the Father the memorial of Christ's death, resurrection, ascension and his coming again on the Last Day, while the people direct their remembrance to the Son. (Unlike us God is eternal, so that past and future events are related to him in exactly the same way as events in the present. For this reason, he can be asked to 'remember' past, present and future.) The priest and people, through their participation in Christ's sacrifice, are brought before the veil of the temple; and, in Christ's name and in the name of the Church, the priest intercedes for the living and the dead, and he rejoices with us in the close relationship we have with the saints. The whole prayer is summed up in the doxology, 'Through him, with him, and in him ...', which expresses our coming into the Father's presence through Christ by the working of the Holy Spirit. The people answer, '*Amen*', which is the most important 'Amen' they ever have to pronounce because it expresses their part in Christ's sacrifice. It expresses the same sentiment as Our Lady on receiving the message of the angel: 'I am the slave of the Lord. May it be done according to your word.' The whole logic and movement of the Eucharistic Prayer leads us to communion, in which we pass through the veil which is Christ's flesh (Heb. 10:20) into the presence of the Father, sharing with Christ his relationship as Son. The result of our intimate union with Christ is that, by the very fact and at the same time, we are organically united to one another as members of Christ's body, the Church; and it is our burden and privilege to be his physical presence on earth, *sent forth* to manifest by our communal life the quality of his love. For this reason, the Eucharist is called the '*Mass*'. As the Catholic Catechism says:

> 1332 [The Eucharist is called] '*Holy Mass*' (*Missa*), because the liturgy in which the mystery of salvation is accomplished concludes with the sending forth (*missio*) of the faithful, so that they may fulfil God's will in their daily lives.

Notes

1. *The Documents of Vatican II* (Geoffrey Chapman, London and Dublin, 1966), p. 141.
2. Ibid.
3. Ibid.
4. See the explanation of *synergy* in ch. 5 below.
5. Nicholas Cabasilas, *The Life in Christ* (St Vladimir's Seminary Press, 1997).
6. *Homily* 17, quoted from *La Epiclesis* by Narciso Lorenzo Leal in *Nova et Vetera* (published by el Monasterio de Benedictinas, Zamorra, Spain), no. 59, January to June, 2005.
7. *Homily on the Treachery of Judas* 1–6, (*PG* 49.380), quoted from Olivier Clément, *The Roots of Christian Mysticism* (New City, 1993), p. 112.

Chapter Five

Ascent and Transformation

There is a Christian document of the first or second century called *The Ascension of Isaiah* which is worth quoting:

> And while he [Isaiah] was speaking with the Holy Spirit in the hearing of them all, he became silent and his mind was taken up from him, and he did not see the men who were standing before him. His eyes were open, but his mouth was shut ... but his breath was still in him for he was seeing a vision. And the angel who was sent to show him [the vision] was not of this firmament nor was he from the angels of the glory of this world, but he came from the seventh heaven. And the people who were standing by, apart from the prophets, did [not] think that the Holy Isaiah had been taken up. And the vision that he saw was not of this world but was from the world that is hidden from the flesh.[1]

This shows a constant theme in Jewish literature immediately before, during and after the time of Christ, the ascension into heaven of a chosen human being who is made capable of knowledge not normally given to men, and is transformed into an angel or a 'son of God' by being in God's presence. God's transforming presence is frequently likened to fire. Anyone who approaches God must pass through a wall of fire and be transformed by it.

Here is a transformation in the third Book of Enoch in which Enoch is turned into an angel:

> When the Holy One, blessed be he, took me to serve the throne of glory... at once my flesh turned to flame, my sinews to blazing fire, my bones to juniper coals, my eyelashes into lightning flashes, my eyeballs to fiery torches, the hairs of my head to hot flames, all my limbs to wings of burning fire and the substance of my body to blazing fire. (3 Enoch 15:1)[2]

Margaret Barker argues that the baptism of Jesus was an ascension experience in this Jewish mystical tradition, that Jesus received the name of Yahweh and became Son of God or was declared Son of God, that his time of temptation in the desert continued this experience, and that he was served by angels and beasts, the four beasts of the Apocalypse. His state as Son of God, of having been transformed by fire so that he was living by the divine life, was made visible at the Transfiguration. Of course, she comes to these conclusions by interpreting the historical documents, while we look at the baptism of Jesus from the point of view of our liturgical celebration of the Christian Mystery which forms an organic whole that can be glimpsed through study and meditation on any part. Hence, it is no surprise to us that there are liturgical texts which place the defeat of the devil and the trampling on the head of Leviathan at Christ's baptism rather than at his death and resurrection. The baptism, death and resurrection of Christ form an indivisible whole, and the Church's theology of baptism has influenced the liturgical account of Christ's baptism, but only because the pattern of his death and resurrection can be seen already in his baptism. As Rowan Williams writes, 'In Jesus, the world of ordinary prosaic time is not destroyed, but it is broken up and reconnected, it works no longer in straight lines but in layers and spirals of meaning.'[3] Nevertheless, it seems to me that Margaret Barker has established a real connection between this Jewish apocalyptic tradition and the Gospel.

This impression is reinforced when we read of the ascension tradition in Eucharistic theology. The very first quotation in this chapter is from *The Ascension of Isaiah*, a very primitive Christian work. Although speaking of Old Testament times, it is really speaking of the Church. The prophets are the Christians, as are the 'faithful who believe in the ascension into heaven'. What ascension is the *Ascension* talking about? Perhaps Alexander Schmemann can give us a clue in a passage on the Eucharist in his book, *The World As Sacrament*:

> The early Christians realized that in order to become the temple of the Holy Spirit, they must ascend to heaven where Christ has ascended. They realized also that this ascension was the very condition of their mission in the world, of their ministry to the world. For there – in heaven – they were immersed in the new life of the Kingdom; and, when after this 'liturgy of ascension', they returned into the world, their faces reflected the light, the 'joy and peace' of that Kingdom and they were truly its witnesses.[4]

If the Eucharist is our ascension into heaven into the presence of the Father through the veil of the body of Christ, then we must expect some reference in liturgical tradition to the transforming effect of fire if there is a connection between the Jewish apocalyptic mysticism and ourselves. Sure enough, it is there: 'We are fed with the bread from heaven, our thirst is quenched by the cup of joy, the chalice afire with the Spirit, the blood wholly warmed by the fire from on high by the Spirit.' The same idea recurs with St Ephraem of Edessa: 'Fire and Spirit are in our baptism. In the bread and the cup also are fire and the Spirit'.[6]

If there is transforming fire in the Eucharist for those who receive it, this must show itself in their ordinary lives.

Ascent and Transformation 61

Here are three testimonies from the Fathers of the Desert:

> Abba Lot came to visit Abba Joseph and said: 'Abba, when I am able, I recite a short office, I fast a little, I pray, I meditate, I stay recollected. As far as I can I try to keep my thought pure. What else should I do?' Then Abba Joseph got up. He stretched out his hands to heaven and his fingers became like burning lamps. He said to Abba Lot, 'If you will, become all fire.'
>
> There was somebody they called Abba Pambo and they said of him that for three years he had begged God saying, 'Do not give me glory in this world.' And God glorified him to the point that no one could look at him in the face because of the glory in it.
>
> A brother came to the cell of Abba Arsenius in Scetis. He looked through the window. He saw the old man as though he were all on fire. (This brother was worthy to see such a thing.)
>
> (*Accounts of the Desert Fathers of the IVth century*)[7]

In case you think this kind of thing happened only in the early Church, here is an account of a visit to St Seraphim of Sarov by N. A. Motovilov in the early nineteenth century. He wanted to know from St Seraphim what is meant by 'acquisition of the Holy Spirit' which St Seraphim taught is the central task of the Christian life. He simply did not understand what St Seraphim was talking about. This part of the interview follows on from his questions and St Seraphim's attempts to answer with words alone:

> 'What I want,' I said, 'is to understand completely.' Then Father Seraphim took me firmly by the shoulders and said to me, 'Right now, good Father, we are both in the Spirit of God. Why, then, do you not look at me?' I

said, 'I cannot look at you now, Father, because lightning flashes from your eyes. Your face has become brighter than the sun, and my eyes ache ...' At these words I looked into his face, and an even greater awe filled me. Picture to yourself the centre of the sun in the most dazzling brightness of its noonday rays, and in this centre is the face of the man who is conversing with you. You see his lips move, you watch the changing expression of his eyes, you hear his voice; you are conscious that someone is holding you by the shoulders. Yet not only do you not see the hands which hold you, but you do not see yourself, nor the man's figure, only the dazzling sphere of light spreading in a radius of many feet, flooding the snow on the field, and the falling sleet, and myself and the great *staretz*. Can one imagine the condition in which I found myself.[8]

From a very different tradition is the mystical experience of St Francis of Assisi when he received the stigmata. Nevertheless, there are common characteristics, all the more striking because of the differences. The accent on flame and light and being consumed and transformed by fire, and the presence of seraphim from heaven indicate that St Bonaventure's account of the event belongs to the same tradition that goes back to the Jewish mystics at the beginnings of the Christian era:

> Because of the many austerities of his previous life and because he had borne Christ's cross continually, he was very much weakened in his body, but in no way in his resolve which made him even more eager to suffer martyrdom. In effect, the fire of his uncontainable love for Jesus had become such a raging furnace that no amount of water, however torrential, could have extinguished the passion of his charity.
> While he was lifting up to God the seraphic ardour of his desires and was transformed by his tender compassion for him who wished to be crucified because

of his extreme love, on the day before the Exaltation of the Holy Cross, while he was praying on the side of the mountain, he saw coming down from the highest heaven a seraphim with six flaming wings that shone brightly. In flight, at enormous speed he came to the spot where the man of God was, and there he remained suspended in the air. Between the wings there appeared the effigy of a crucified man whose hands and feet were extended as though nailed to a cross. Two wings were lifted over the head, two were used for flying, and two covered his whole body.

Before this apparition the saint was overcome with amazement, and he felt in his heart a joy mixed with sorrow. In effect he rejoiced at the gracious way that Christ, who was in the form of a seraphim, looked at him; while, at the same time, the sight of him nailed to a cross pierced his soul like a painful sword.

He was filled with wonder at such a mysterious vision, knowing that the pain of the passion in no way could bear comparison with the immortal joy of the seraphim. At last, the Lord gave him to understand that this vision had been given by divine Providence so that the friend of God would know beforehand that he must be transformed totally into the image of Christ crucified, not by a martyrdom in the flesh, but by his spirit being totally consumed by fire. It happened in this way, that when the vision disappeared, he was left with a marvelous warmth in his heart, in no way less marvelous than the signs that were imprinted on his body.[9]

This total transformation by which mere creatures are brought into the divine life of the Trinity as sons of God is the effect of the sacraments. We are introduced into the process by baptism and our transformation takes place because we become one with Christ in the Eucharist. The agent of this change is the Holy Spirit who so unites us with Christ that we experience our baptism when we are ready for it by conversion, and communion by contemplation. Just as St Seraphim saw the Spirit come down on the bread and wine in the form of fire and later became transformed by fire himself, just as St Francis so wanted to be united by love to Christ in his sacrifice that he was transformed interiorly and bore the marks of Christ's wounds, so we share in the same Spirit by which the bread and wine become Christ's body and blood, and we become one with Christ in his sacrifice, every time we go to Mass. They are shining examples of what we are destined to become, of what the Eucharist is doing to us invisibly in so far as we let the Spirit work. They provide the vision: we, in celebrating Mass, make visible to the world something of what is happening to us through the quality of our love.

Notes

1. Quoted from Margaret Barker, *The Risen Lord* (T. & T. Clark, 1996).
2. Quoted from Margaret Barker, *The Gate of Heaven* (SPCK, 1991), p. 173.
3. Rowan Williams, *The Dwelling of the Light* (Canterbury Press, Norwich, 2003), p. 8.
4. Alexander Schmemann, *The World As Sacrament* (Darton, Longman & Todd, 1966), p. 31ff
5. An anonymous homily inspired by St Hippolytus' *Treatise on Easter*, Exordium 8, taken from Olivier Clément, *The Roots of Christian Mysticism*, p. 113.
6. St Ephraem *On Faith* (Lamy I, p. 413) from Clément, *Roots*, p. 113.
7. See also *The Sayings of the Desert Fathers*, trans. Benedicta Ward (Cistercian Publications, 1975), pp. 103, 196 and 13.
8. *The Conversation of St Seraphim with N. A. Motovilov*. This is a small part of a long conversation. All of it is worthwhile, and very beautiful. See also V. Zander, *St Seraphim of Sarov* (SPCK, 1975), pp. 90ff.
9. Translated from *Leyenda Mayor* by St Bonaventure, XIII, Las Sacradas Llagas, in *San Francis de Asis* (Biblioteca de Aurores Cristinos, Madrid, 2000).

Chapter Six

The Twofold Gift of the Spirit

There is a clear and necessary connection between the coming of the kingdom and the need for a radical change of attitude which is called 'conversion' or 'repentance' in the Gospels. 'Repent, for the kingdom of heaven has come near,' is the first message of Jesus to the Jews. It became the function of the Holy Spirit to make present the kingdom and also to so transform those who are open to such a change through repentance to enable them to receive what God is offering them, nothing less than a share in his own divine life. This is the twofold gift of the Spirit who operates in the sacraments: firstly, the objective gift of salvation in Christ, of being scooped up to share in the divine life, and, secondly, the subjective ability to benefit from it.

In the Eastern tradition the sacraments have an objective and a subjective dimension: there is an insistence that, normally speaking, we should be conscious of the Spirit's action in us and be able freely to cooperate, especially in the great sacraments of baptism and communion. There needs to be what the Greeks call *synergy*[1] between the free action of the Spirit and the freedom of human beings. The usage of the word in the Christian East includes: a) the synergy of the three divine persons of the Trinity, b) the synergy of the divine and human wills in the one person of Christ, c) the synergy of grace and free will in the life of the believer, d) the synergy of the Holy

66 *Heaven Revealed*

Spirit and the Church in the liturgy.

The Church opposed the Monothelite heresy which was condemned by the Sixth Ecumenical Council (Constantinople III) in AD 680 precisely because, by proposing only one divine–human will in Christ, the heretics threatened the doctrine that salvation involves the harmony between the divine and human wills acting freely together, firstly in Christ and then in us. This harmony between the divine will and the human will was lost at the Fall and was only re-established in Jesus by his life of obedience unto death, which is the life of the Incarnation. Of course, his Spirit acted in the world before Christ's coming; so there were many saints in the Old Testament whose sanctity was a reflection of him who had not yet become man. This harmony between God's will and that of human beings, brought about by Christ's Spirit, is passed on to the Church which is Christ's body; and it is the outstanding characteristic of the liturgy which is the Church's prayer. In our turn, by living in Christ, our own wills can come to work in *synergy* with God's will, thus making it possible for us to share in the divine life too. Fr Jean Corbon, a Greek Catholic priest and theologian from the Lebanon who made a major contribution to the official Catholic Catechism, wrote:

> Readers will understand my preferring 'synergy' to 'cooperation' (an equivalent term derived from Latin), since the connotations of the latter are quite different in the modern languages. The 'synergy' of the Holy Spirit and the Church is a key idea for an understanding of the mystery of the liturgy. It has its foundation in Christ himself. Being true God and true man, Jesus has two wills (contrary to the Monothelite heresy) and two operations or 'energies' (contrary to the Monoenergist heresy), which de facto are in unison but freely so and without confusion. Thus Christian sanctity is wholly located in the divinization of our nature in Christ ... through the union of our wills with that of the Father

in Christ and through the 'synergy' of the baptized and the Holy Spirit in every vital action. This union of wills is love in operation ... (Corbon, p. 192, n. 1)[2]

St Thomas puts it this way: 'Charity is not something created in the soul, but is the Holy Ghost Himself, dwelling in the mind' (IIa-IIae, q. 23, a. 2, resp). Our love becomes by our free collaboration a reflection of his. From the point of view of the subjective experience of those participating in the liturgy, and especially in the Mass, the Holy Spirit's action is fourfold. Firstly, the Spirit *prepares* us to participate. It could be said that his work begins in our houses as we are making ready to go to Mass. If we allow him, he will prepare our minds and hearts to receive Christ, as he prepared the children of Israel for the coming of Christ. Secondly, he 'will *teach* you everything and remind you of all I have said to you'. (John 14:26) This he does when, through the reading or the sermon or through some other experience, the word of God becomes alive and we see it as urgently addressed to us, so that we act on it. The third way is expressed in the *epiclesis* at Mass: we are introduced into the *Christian Mystery* and come to share in the death and resurrection of Christ through the Holy Spirit. We examined this in the first three chapters. To the extent that we are receptive to the Holy Spirit's action, to dying so that we may rise with Christ, the Holy Spirit acts in a fourth way: he brings us into *communion* with Christ. We come into communion with Christ through the infinite Gift of love of the Father for the Son and the Son for the Father which is the Holy Spirit. As the doxology of the Mass says, through our oneness with Christ in the unity of the Holy Spirit, we are brought into the presence of the Father who is the Source and Goal of the Blessed Trinity, of the liturgy, and of the Christian life.

We must be on the Spirit's wavelength for the grace to flow. This synergy does not always coincide with the celebration of the rite. Thus the full effect of the sacrament may very well happen at another time, in circumstances which seem far removed from the celebration. Conversion belongs to baptism, and contemplation belongs to the Eucharist as dimensions of the same reality, brought about by the same Spirit, but the moment of conversion or contemplation may not coincide with the reception of the sacrament. Just as conversion can happen before baptism, during baptism or, in the case of those baptized in infancy, at an appropriate moment in life after baptism, so contemplation can happen before communion, during communion, or after communion. For this reason, the connexion between conversion and baptism, and contemplation and communion, is often not recognized. People have even been known to oppose external ritual to internal spiritual experience. What connects conversion with baptism, and contemplation with communion, is the gift of the Spirit, symbolized by the *anointing* with Chrism in baptism and by the *epiclesis* over the gifts and over the people in the Mass; but the Spirit's action which is a response to the Church's prayer during the celebration is not limited by time or space. Thus, as Paul Evdokimov puts it, the ascetical and mystical lives are an appropriation by the Christian of the Church's sacramental life.

According to some Greek Fathers, infant baptism makes a baptismal experience of conversion later in life necessary. It takes many forms: for some it is dramatic and for others it is gradual. It goes under several names. The Greek Fathers called it 'Baptism in the Spirit', 'Second Baptism', 'Baptism of Repentance', and 'Baptism of Tears'. However, for western Catholics, it is perhaps better to avoid using for this experience any name which seems to cast doubt on the effectiveness of infant baptism. It can be called 'conversion', 'renewal in the Spirit', 'experience of our baptism', or 'a decisive meeting with the risen Lord' (John Paul II). St Symeon the New Theologian (949–1022) of Constantinople uses identical arguments to modern Pentecostals in favour of 'Baptism in the Spirit', though the outward sign of the Spirit's inward action is for him tears rather than tongues, tears which are the sign that the person's hardness of heart has melted. Through the Spirit's action, tears of sorrow for sin and for our hardness of heart against the love of God are turned into tears of joy at the Spirit's indwelling in the soul, and the Christian basks in God's love. It is the baptismal experience of death and resurrection, a question of subjectively appropriating what is given at Baptism. It is the radical change of attitude that Jesus required from his listeners so that they could take advantage of the coming of God's kingdom, something that has to be done time and time again.

Of the Eucharist Nicholas Cabasilas (d. *c*.1370), a layman, nephew of the Archbishop of Thessalonika who was also a noted theologian, and one of the greatest liturgical theologians in history, wrote: 'It is impossible to go beyond it ... after the Eucharist there is nothing to be striven for: one has to stop there.'[3] How can we go beyond becoming 'bones of Christ's bones, flesh of Christ's flesh, one body with Christ' in communion? St Paul likens our sacramental union with Christ to marriage. If this is so, if there is nothing beyond union with Christ in the Eucharist, what about contemplation and mystical marriage as experienced by such saints as St Teresa of Avila and St John of the Cross? Are they not forms of union with Christ far closer, more sanctifying and more complete than what we receive in sacramental communion? What about being transfigured by the divine light, as Jesus was on Mount Tabor and as has happened to many Eastern saints? What is the relationship between these 'subjective' experiences and the reception of Holy Communion? The Catholic Professor Zaehner wrote, 'Every time we go to Holy Communion, so long as we are in a state of grace, we share in God's own godhead – we are "deified". We are not conscious of it: the mystic is. Therein lies the difference.'[4] Eastern theology confirms this view. Just as the experience of conversion is baptismal, so the experience of contemplation and even mystical union is Eucharistic, even though the contemplative experience may seem unconnected to the celebration of the Mass. The Father sends the Spirit to make the bread and wine the body and blood of Christ, and Christ is the very source of the Spirit for us. The Holy Spirit is also invoked to transform us into Christ's body through receiving the divinized body and blood of Christ. According to Fr Jean Corbon,[5] this the Holy Spirit can do in so far as we let him. When we receive Christ in communion, the Holy Spirit who is in him prolongs our communion long after the species of bread and wine have been digested, transforming us into him and remaining with us just as long as we allow him to stay. Although this presence of Christ is no longer dependent on the presence of the 'accidents' of bread and wine which disintegrate in the stomach, but on the Holy Spirit, it is a principal effect of the Eucharist and is therefore truly Eucharistic. The whole purpose of communion is our permanent transformation into Christ, to become one body with him long after the 'accidents' have disappeared. This truth can be obscured when our theological explanation forgets that the presence of Christ's body and blood in the form of bread and wine is wholly dependent on the Spirit making effective Christ's words, and that Christ's continued presence in us, after the sacramental action is over, also depends on the Holy Spirit.

St Gregory Palamas wrote these inspiring words:

> Since the Son of God, in his incomparable love for men, did not only unite his divine Hypostasis with our nature, by clothing himself in a living body and a soul gifted with intelligence ... but also united himself ... with the human hypostases themselves, in mingling himself with each of the faithful by communion with his Holy Body, and since he becomes one single body with us and makes us a temple of the undivided Divinity, for in the very body of Christ dwelleth the fullness of the Godhead bodily (Col. 2:9), how should he not illumi-

nate those who commune worthily with the divine ray of his Body which is within us, lightening their souls, as he illuminated the very bodies of the disciples on Mount Tabor? For, on the day of the Transfiguration, that Body, source of the light of grace, was not yet united with our bodies; it illuminated from outside those who worthily approached it, and sent the illumination into the soul by the intermediary of the physical eyes; but now, since it is mingled with us and exists in us it illuminates the soul from within.[6]

Contemplation can be experienced before the Eucharist and can lead up to it. Once there was a hermit in the Egyptian desert who had spent many years far from the sacraments but in deep contemplation. When he knew himself to be dying, he decided to make the journey to Alexandria to attend Mass and receive communion. When he received communion he was transfigured by the light of the Holy Spirit so that no one could look at him,[7] and he died in ecstasy, the one communion making his life of contemplation complete, bringing him into the Presence of the Father in heaven. For him, contemplation was a lifelong preparation for that communion.

Contemplation can be experienced during the Eucharist. St Symeon would insist to his monks that they would only receive communion worthily if reception were accompanied by contemplation. We must remember he is speaking to monks; and he requires only that level of prayer which he expects all monks to attain in a life dedicated to God. He writes:

> If you partake in pure contemplation of what you have taken, then you have become worthy of such a table. When we eat of it and have in ourselves no more fruit than from eating corporeal food, without gaining in awareness of another life, we have received merely bread and not God at all.[8]

We must remember that St Symeon did not live among people who denied the Catholic teaching of the Eucharist, so he could afford to exaggerate. He is not denying the objective consecration of the bread and wine: he is only saying that, without insight of faith, we cannot penetrate beyond the outward sign. St Maximos the Confessor sees progress in prayer in eucharistic terms, as an ever deeper communion. He wrote:

> Whoever passes from ascesis to inner freedom is able to contemplate in the Holy Spirit the truth of creatures and things. It is as if he passed from the flesh of Christ to his soul. Another, through this symbolic contemplation of the world, passes to the more naked mystical initiation that is 'theology'. It is as if he passed from the soul of Christ to his spirit. Another, through this state, is mystically led to the ineffable state where all definition is overridden by a radical negation. It is as if he passed from the spirit of Christ to his divinity.[9]

Contemplation can be experienced after the Eucharist or apart from the Eucharist, but it is always a personal experience of that intimate relationship between Christ and the Church that is brought about by the Eucharist, a response by God to the prayer to send the Holy Spirit to make us one in Christ.

Of course, this experience is not automatic: we cannot share in a contemplative experience of Christ's presence in the Spirit if we do not leave behind all worldly cares and preoccupations, or, at least, let them fade into the background so that we may concentrate on him whom we are receiving. We are called to do this when the priest tells us to 'Lift up your hearts', and we say we are doing this when we reply, 'We have lifted them up to the Lord'. In this connection let us quote again the late Fr Alexander Schmemann, this time more fully:

> The liturgy of the Eucharist is best understood as a

journey or procession. It is a journey of the Church into the dimension of the kingdom ... The liturgy begins then as a real separation from the world. In our attempt to make Christianity appeal to the man on the street, we have often minimized, or even completely forgotten, this necessary separation. We always want to make Christianity 'understandable' and 'acceptable' to this mythical 'modern' man on the street. And we forget that the Christ of whom we speak is 'not of this world' and that after his resurrection he was not recognized even by his own disciples ... The early Christians realized that in order to become a temple of the Holy Spirit, they must ascend into heaven where Christ has ascended. They realized also that this ascension was the very condition of their mission in the world, of their ministry to the world. For there – in heaven – they were immersed in the new life of the Kingdom; and when after this 'liturgy of ascension', they returned into the world, their faces reflected the light, the 'joy and peace' of that Kingdom and they were truly its witnesses. They brought no programmes and no theories; but wherever they went, the seeds of the Kingdom sprouted, faith was kindled, life was transfigured, things impossible were made possible ... In church today, we so often find we meet only the same old world, not Christ and his kingdom. We do not realize that we never get anywhere because we never leave any place behind us.[10]

After the celebration, to the degree that we have been transformed by our communion with Christ, we will be able to tackle the problems of this world in such a way that Christ acts through us. In St John's Gospel, Jesus charges St Peter with an important role among his disciples; but he first asks, 'Do you love me more than these' (John 21:15). Our relationship with Christ is what makes our mission in the world qualitatively different. Unless we are content to practise a ministry devoid of this Christian quality, we must strive to reach a balance between prayer and work in which our prayer does not suffer. Only when we are so transformed by grace that the difference between prayer and work is transcended by our utter dedication to God, there will be regular times when we have to leave the world to its own devices and seek God alone.

Just as Baptism is incomplete in the adult without the experience of conversion, so in the Eastern tradition our reception of Communion is incomplete without contemplation; though with some, the purifying process that leads to contemplation may have to wait until the next life. This can be put in another way: in spite of great differences in temperaments and vocations, under normal circumstances all baptized are called to conversion and all communicants are called to contemplation; and conversion leads on to contemplation as baptism leads us to the Eucharist. The Fathers of the Desert set out to be contemplatives, not because they sought a vocation radically different from that of anyone else, but because they wanted to remove from their path those obstacles which keep coming up in ordinary life and impede this natural progression from conversion to contemplation, through tears to joy. It is the Holy Spirit who brings this about if we let him, when and as he wants, and he probably does so with people in all kinds of walks of life far more often than we realize. I am sure there are many contemplatives who have never even heard of contemplation and would be surprised to know that is what they are doing.

This link between communion and contemplation means that, in the Eastern tradition, it would be impossible to divide religious into 'active' and 'contemplative' orders, even though there are monks and nuns who are hermits and others who are engaged in pastoral work and other Christian activities, because contemplation is open to everybody who communicates, and all who are free to do so must so order their lives that contemplation becomes possible. If it is not possible today, it will be tomorrow or when God wishes. An active life that does not lead to contemplation is a stunted Christian life, not a different vocation.

For the Orthodox East, as among the western Fathers of the Church like St Gregory the Great, the contemplative life is the goal of the Christian life on earth, a foretaste of the joys of heaven; and the active life is all that we do to prepare ourselves for it, all the duties that we have to fulfil according to our particular vocation. These may involve apostolic works, caring for the sick, teaching in schools; but they also include keeping silence within a cloister, singing divine office, fasting, praying and penance. All these belong to the active life because they are all what we do in God's service. Contemplation is God's gift to us, when we are ready for it. In the same tradition, the Jesuits claim that they are 'contemplatives in action'; and Mother Teresa of Calcutta reminded her sisters that, although they are swept off their feet by their service to the poorest of the poor, their vocation is a contemplative one. They must meet Christ in the streets, the same Christ that they adore in the Blessed Sacrament. Pope John Paul II said that to have a truly effective ministry in this secular world, we must become contemplatives. God is present in every situation, at every moment; and all it needs to tune into that presence and to remain conscious of it is purity of heart. No Christian vocation has a monopoly on that. As Carlo Carretto used to say, the level of our Christian life is the level of our prayer; and this is true, whatever our vocation. In a secular world that knows nothing of genuine Christian experience and does not automatically accept as true the teaching of the Church, it is all the more important that we Christians who attempt to bear witness to Jesus, either by our absence from the world in the desert or cloister, or by our presence within the world, should have our witness reinforced by a contemplative relationship with God. Third-hand religion is too abstract for most people and won't convince them anyway.

Of course, if we accept the link between communion and contemplation, this should influence the way we celebrate Mass. A Mass that is so busy that it positively impedes any contemplative reception of Christ in the depth of each heart is just as unliturgical and unbalanced as a Mass which impedes communal participation. There must be something to encourage the participants to meet Christ in the depths of the soul as they receive him into their mouths in communion. One of the most impressive things about Mass in the Charismatic Renewal is how very active and joyous singing can lead people into an intense silence after communion, a silence that is communal and individual at the same time. I am not saying that all Masses should be like that. The style and the means used may be very different: suitable music, well sung, can induce people to silence; a few well chosen words and some training can be effective; but whatever means is used, a good liturgy will always encourage those who take part to interiorize what they outwardly celebrate, and will invite them to welcome Christ into the very depths of their soul; and a bad liturgy has so much noise on the surface that no one can enter into his heart and recognize there, let alone enjoy, the presence of Christ whom he has received.

Notes

1. See Cassian Folsom OSB, monk of St Meinrad's Abbey, Indiana, USA, 'The Holy Spirit and the Church in the Liturgy', in he *Homiletic and Pastoral Review*. Much of the information on 'synergy' is based on this article, as are the quotations from Jean Corbon.
2. Jean Corbon, *The Wellspring of Worship* (Paulist Press, New York, 1988), quoted from the article by Cassian Folsom OSB: see note 1 above.
3. Nicholas Cabasilas, *The Life in Christ* (St Vladimir's Seminary Press, 1997).
4. *The Catholic Church and World Religions*, p. 18, quoted from E. L. Mascall, *The Christian Universe* (Darton, Longman & Todd, 1966), p. 84.
5. See Corbon, *Wellspring* above.
6. *Triads*, quoted from John Meyendorff, *A Study of Gregory Palamas*

(Faith Press, 1964), p. 151.
7. See ch. 5 above for more on union with God as 'fire' and 'light'.
8. Hilarion Alfeyev, *St Symeon the New Theologian and Orthodox Tradition* (Oxford Early Christian Studies, OUP, 2000), p. 89. I cannot praise this book too highly.
9. Maximos the Confessor, *Ambigua* 91, 1560
10 Alexander Schmemann, *The World As Sacrament* (Darton, Longman & Todd, 1965), pp. 29ff.

Chapter Seven

Epiclesis

> Along with the anamnesis, the epiclesis
> is at the heart of each sacramental celebration,
> most especially of the Eucharist.
> *Catechism of the Catholic Church* §1106

Until the new Eucharistic prayers came into use after Vatican II, the epiclesis was not really a western concern, and the role of the Holy Spirit was rarely invoked as a factor in our understanding of the sacraments. In the West, the emphasis has been on consecration, with Christ as the Consecrator and the priest as his instrument. Theologians knew that Christ consecrates by the power of the Spirit, but the Spirit's role was not brought to the fore because the emphasis was on *Christ's* power which has been given to the priest. In the East, on the other hand, they have always been very conscious of the important part the Holy Spirit plays in our sanctification in general and in the sacraments in particular. For the Orthodox East, the liturgy is the place where Christ's promise is fulfilled that 'I will ask the Father, and he will give you another Advocate, to be with you forever. This is the Spirit of truth, whom the world cannot receive' (John

---

All the quotations from Eastern and other liturgies are taken and translated from the article 'La Epiclesis' by Narciso Lorenxo Leal (see note 8 to chapter 5 above).

14:16–17). The priest's power is the power to *ask* the Father in Christ's name, in full confidence that the Father will do what is asked because of the new covenant between God and his People. This emphasis on the action of the Holy Spirit enabled the Eastern tradition to understand the connection between the sacraments, especially Baptism and the Eucharist, and other dimensions of the Christian life. The epiclesis manifests the priest's utter weakness and dependence on God, as well as his greatness and what he can do with God's help. On the other hand, the Western emphasis on the presence and action of Christ has engendered its own spirituality and has been a major factor in the formation of many saints. It has also enabled the Western church to develop adoration of the Blessed Sacrament, which I am sure will one day be seen as a gain both for East and West, once we discover our unity and cease to criticize the differences between us. The truth is that the Eastern and Western theologies are complementary and look at the consecration in the Mass from different perspectives.

The consecration is effected by all the three Persons of the Blessed Trinity, as the tradition of the epiclesis bears witness, but the Persons' relationships to the one divine act differ according to their relationships within the Blessed Trinity and their relationships with us. Both the Eastern and the Western traditions become lopsided when they are not balanced by each other. In Western thought, the Trinitarian structure of the Mass was accepted, preserved, but tended to be forgotten at a devotional level, because little emphasis was put on the activity of the Spirit, until the balance was restored in the reforms after Vatican II by means of the epiclesis.

In the early Church, no one thought of a particular moment during the Eucharistic Prayer when the consecration of the bread and wine took place: the whole Prayer was consecratory. Indeed, *consecration* was not uppermost in the minds of the early Christians because, for people who interpreted the Eucharist primarily as a *theophany*, consecration was simply a means to that end, and their attention was absorbed by what was being signified rather than by the sign itself. The epiclesis was normally placed after the *anamnesis* (memorial) of the Last Supper, the death and resurrection of Christ, and thus followed the pattern of Jewish table prayers which placed intercessions after the remembrance of God's mighty deeds. It was a prayer, usually addressed to the Father to send his Spirit, though we shall see an example of an epiclesis being addressed to Christ. It usually asked for the transformation of the bread and wine into the body and blood of Christ and for the transformation of the people participating in the Eucharist, so that they become one body in Christ, with those gifts necessary for people who wish to participate in the divine life. In the Alexandrian and Roman traditions, the 'petition for consecration' is before the words of Institution, 'This is my body ... This is the chalice of my blood ...'; and the petition that communion should be effective is placed afterwards. The epiclesis was inserted in the Eucharistic Prayer to clarify for the faithful what the whole Eucharistic Prayer, and even the whole celebration, is about, rather than to provide a moment of consecration. The same was also true of the words of Institution which belong to the part of the Eucharistic Prayer in which God's mighty deeds are commemorated. Centuries later, when the question about the exact moment of consecration had been asked, there was an unfortunate controversy between East and West as to when the moment of consecration takes place. Obviously there is a moment when ordinary bread and wine become the body and blood of Christ. However, it may differ from rite to rite.

One of the earliest examples of an epiclesis is that of St Hippolytus, one of the presbyters of Rome, who gives this as an example of how a Eucharistic Prayer should be, according to the Apostolic Tradition. When it was written, bishops composed their own Eucharistic Prayer, but according to a strict pattern that had been handed down, and Hippolytus is presenting us with this pattern. Thus the words of the prayer may never have been used exactly as they were written. It has had a powerful influence down the centuries, and our own Eucharistic Prayer II is based on it. I believe that the epiclesis of St Hippolytus has enormous ecclesiological and ecumenical significance in our own day:

> And we ask that you send your Holy Spirit on to the oblation of holy Church, bringing it together in one, and that you give to all who receive these holy gifts the fullness of the Holy Spirit, for the confirmation of the faith in truth, that we may praise and glorify you through your servant (*puerum*) Jesus Christ: through whom ... (doxology)

Jeremy Driscoll OSB, in a very valuable work, *Theology at the Eucharistic Table*,[1] gives a detailed study of these words, making use of the best scholarship available. Because he is chiefly concerned with the relationship between the teaching of the Church and the celebration of the Eucharist, he concentrates on the phrase, 'the fullness of the holy Spirit, for the confirmation of the faith in truth, that we may praise and glorify you'.

We have already seen the text from St John's Gospel, 'And I will ask the Father, and he will give you another Advocate to be with you for ever. This is the Spirit of truth, whom the world cannot receive' (John 14:16–17). Join this text with another one from St Luke's Gospel, 'If you then, who are evil, know how to give good gifts to your children, how much more will your heavenly Father give the Holy Spirit to those who ask him?' (Luke 11:13). In this text from St Hippolytus, he who presides at the Eucharist is asking the Father for the Holy Spirit, the Spirit of truth, to confirm the faith of the participants in truth so that, as one single body, they may give true worship, true praise and glory to the Father. This shows the Eucharist to be, in the words of Vatican II, the *source* and *summit* of the Christian life. Remember that the epiclesis is not a solitary 'word of power': it is really expressing a dimension of the whole Eucharistic Prayer and, to a certain extent, of the whole celebration. The Eucharist calls down the Holy Spirit to make us one with Christ and to give us a true understanding of our faith, so that we may offer to God true praise and glory in the Eucharist. Indeed, we offer with God the Son his own praise and glory to the Father. That is our contribution to the salvation of mankind.

In this epiclesis we are in the world of the early Fathers who had to deal with sects and heresies. In fact this vocabulary is identical to that of St Irenaeus (d. *c*.170) who claims:

> The Church's preaching is the same everywhere and remains true to itself, supported by the witness of the prophets, the apostles and all the disciples, from the beginning, through the middle, to the end, in a word, throughout the history of God's constant activity of saving humanity and making himself present to us in faith. This faith never ceases. We receive it from the Church and guard it under the action of the Spirit like a precious liquid that rejuvenates itself and the vessel containing it. The Church has been entrusted with this gift of God, just as God gave his breath to the flesh that he fashioned in order that all the members might receive its life. And this gift conveys the fullness of union with Christ, that is, the Holy Spirit, pledge of incorruptibility, confirmation of our faith, ladder of our ascent to God ... For where the Church is, there the Spirit of God is also, and where the Spirit of God is, there the Church is, and all grace. And the Spirit is truth.[2]

According to St Irenaeus, the Catholic Church alone has the *charisma veritatis*, the charism of truth, because the Church alone has the Holy Spirit. Because the Church has the Spirit who is the key for understanding the Scriptures, it can see the true pattern which reveals Christ's face in the Bible. St Irenaeus likens the Scriptures to a mosaic of a king. The small pieces which represent the texts of the Bible all combine to reveal Christ. A heretic is someone who rearranges the pieces to make a mosaic of a fox, and claims that it is the same mosaic because he uses the same pieces. St Irenaeus says that the heretic may use the same texts; but he lacks the key to putting them in the right order, because only the Church has its faith confirmed in the truth by the Spirit. Without the Holy Spirit it is not the same book.

The Gnostics' claims that they had secret knowledge and secret scriptures, such as the *Gospel of Judas* which has recently been discovered, were rejected out of hand, and the living, public voice of the Church was opposed to it, a voice guided by the Spirit of God. The Gospel of Jesus Christ was proclaimed publicly, and the apostles preached and taught in public, and their message is publicly proclaimed and commonly understood in all Catholic churches. Individual local churches could go wrong and forfeit this guidance, but not the universal Church. Churches and people should be prepared to be guided by the churches that owe their foundation to the apostles, and most especially by the Church of Rome where Saints Peter and Paul were martyred and which is in contact with churches throughout the world. Irenaeus wrote:

> With this Church [of Rome], because of its pre-eminent origin, every Church must necessarily be in agreement, that is to say, the faithful everywhere. For therein has been preserved for all time, to the benefit of all, the Tradition that comes from the apostles.[3]

It is the common teaching of the early Fathers that the unity of the Church is dependent on the Spirit, and where the Spirit is present, you will find the Catholic Faith manifested in a common understanding of Christian Revelation. This is not a position invented by the Emperor Constantine and his cronies who sought to unify the empire with their version of Christian Revelation. It is the position of St Irenaeus in the second century, of Origen not long afterwards, and of all the Catholic Fathers both before and after Constantine was born. In modern times, the Catholic, Orthodox and Oriental churches hold this same position. It is this general agreement which forms the context and basis of our divergent understandings of the Church's teaching authority. Each church or group of churches has interpreted this common tradition in the light of its own history, so that the understanding of each must be seen within the context of this tradition, and, without denying our own traditions which reflect what the Holy Spirit has taught us down the centuries, it is time to find a solution to our differences which is wider than our own history and takes into account the lessons learnt from the same Spirit in the other churches.

In accordance with this tradition, the epiclesis of St Hippolytus asks for the Holy Spirit to descend on the offerings and on the people, so that the Church may be one, united in the same understanding of the Christian Mystery, which is the effect of the Spirit's action. This allows them to offer true worship to God. There is an intimate and reciprocal relationship between the Church's understanding of Christian truth and the celebration of the Eucharist in which the Spirit is invoked on the Church. In the words of St Irenaeus, 'As far as we are concerned, our thinking accords with the Eucharist, and the Eucharist in turn confirms our thinking.' For St Hippolytus and St Irenaeus, the source of the Church's unity of belief and unique teaching authority is the Holy Spirit who comes down on the gifts and on the assembly in the Eucharist, an assembly that exists because it has received the apostles' good news through the ministry of the word.

A very primitive Eucharistic Prayer where traces of

Jewish table prayers can still be seen is found in the *Apostolic Constitutions*, a fourth-century collection of earlier liturgical materials. Here is its epiclesis:

> We beseech you to look with a benign eye on the gifts which we present before you, O God who needs nothing, and that you should find them agreeable in honour of your Christ.
> Send your Holy Spirit, the Witness to the sufferings of the Lord Jesus, on this sacrifice, and let it become manifest that this bread is the body of your Christ and this chalice the blood of your Christ, so that those who participate may be confirmed in piety, may obtain pardon for sins, may be freed from the devil and his seductions, may receive the fullness of the Holy Spirit, that they may be worthy of your Christ and reach eternal life, and that you, Omnipotent Lord, may be reconciled with them.[4]

Before commenting, here is the epiclesis from the earliest version of the Liturgy of St Basil, which may have been written directly by his hand (fourth century):

> We place before you the symbols (*antitypes*) of the holy body and blood of your Christ, and we ask and invoke you, Holy of holies, for your merciful goodness, that the Holy Spirit come on us and on these gifts placed before you: that he bless and sanctify, and make manifest that this bread is the very body of our Lord, God and Saviour Jesus Christ. And that this chalice is truly the most precious blood of our Lord, God and Saviour, Jesus Christ. The same is poured out for the life of the world. And for all of us who share in the one bread and the one cup, that we may be united with one another in the communion of the unique Holy Spirit. That our participation in the holy body and blood of your Christ will never be a cause of judgement and condemnation; rather that we may find mercy and grace in union with

all the saints who have pleased you in every generation: with our ancestors, the fathers, the patriarchs, with the prophets, the apostles, the preachers, the evangelists, the martyrs, the confessors, with the doctors and all the souls of the just who died in the faith; specially with the most holy, pure and blessed for her outstanding excellence, Our Lady and Mother of God and ever-Virgin Mary.[5]

Hence, the Holy Spirit is witness to the sufferings of Christ and makes manifest that the bread is the body and the wine is the blood of Christ so that those who participate are confirmed in piety, receive the forgiveness of sins and are freed from the devil, and receive the fullness of the Spirit. We are united by the Holy Spirit to one another and with all the saints, all who have died, including the apostles and the Virgin Mary, Mother of God. The epiclesis emphasizes the infinite power of God at work in the Mass, but also the complete and utter *dependence* of the Church on God's Spirit for it to function as a church.

It has been noticed that these early examples of the epiclesis do not ask that the bread and wine be changed into the body and blood of Christ as in many other epicleses. The Eucharistic Prayer of St Hippolytus, for instance, merely asks that the Spirit be sent on the Church's oblation, without specifying what happens to the oblation. The Eucharistic Prayers which have been quoted ask the Father to send his Spirit to *make manifest* the bread as the body of Christ and the wine as the blood of Christ. It has been said that the Church had not yet developed a satisfactory language to describe what is happening at the consecration. I beg to differ. The authors know exactly what they are asking for, and they put their request very succinctly. Of course, their petition to the Father implies a necessary change of bread and wine into the body and blood of Christ; but this is not uppermost in their minds; it is not what engages their attention. In St John's theology both God the Father and his Son were glorified by the cross because the crucifixion made manifest God's true nature as self-giving Love. Although Jesus was with his disciples always until the end of the world, Christ *manifested* his presence among them in his appearances after the resurrection. This is very clear in St Luke's story of the disciples on the way to Emmaus. Jesus was present with them on their way, but *manifested* his presence to them in the breaking of bread. For the authors of these epicleses, the Mass is a *theophany* made possible by the Holy Spirit, in which God the Father manifests his Presence to the Church through his Son who, in turn, is manifesting his presence in the act by which he hands himself over to us to be our food and drink. In the Mass, the Church is brought into the Presence of the Father through the temple veil which is the flesh of Christ (Heb. 10:19–20), this being possible only because Christ has died, once and for all, on the cross. The Sanctus is a characteristic prayer of the angels in theophanies (Isaiah 6:6; Rev. 4:8); and the 'Benedictus qui venit' from Psalm 117 implies the presence of the Messiah. This prayer is both a request that God be manifest and that we should recognize Christ's presence in the Breaking of Bread. They do not direct their attention towards how this comes about.

The final edition of the Eucharistic Prayer of St Basil has changed the phrase 'Make manifest that this bread is the very body of our Lord God and Saviour the Lord Jesus Christ ...' and now asks that he 'make[s] the bread into the very body ...' We are not among those who claim that the most primitive position is the most authentic one, nor are we among those who adopt later solutions to the detriment of those in the past: we are Catholics who believe that the Holy Spirit brings forth new things and old in every generation. We expect change, but we also expect consistency; and we look into the past to seek aspects of the truth we may have forgotten, and we look at the present to give us new insights into the Christian Mystery, the Mystery that has been proclaimed without substantial change since the beginning of the Church.

Hence, 'make manifest' reminds us that the Eucharist is a theophany in which God in Christ manifests himself as gift through symbols. The word 'symbol' comes from a Greek word *symballein* which means 'to throw together or to unite', and is used in the sense of two realities which are united in such a way that one owes its significance to the other and becomes the means of participating in the other. Hence, Jesus Christ is *the* symbol, because in him God and man are united so that his human nature manifests a divine Person, and through him we share in the divine life. Bread and wine are placed in the context by which their only meaning is to manifest the body and blood of Christ, this being an *objective* change because it is brought about by God. However, when the Church had to stress the reality of the bread and wine before the consecration and the reality of Christ's body and blood after the consecration against heretics who believed matter to be evil and the body of Christ to be a mere appearance, then the reality of the *change* from bread and wine into the body and blood of Christ hit the Christian imagination and eventually came to be expressed in the epiclesis.

There are two petitions in the epiclesis which, though they are distinct, belong to one another. The first in the petition for *consecration* and the second is for a change in the Christians taking part so that they may benefit from *communion* with the Eucharistic Christ. This corresponds to the double message of Christ: firstly the Good News that God's kingdom is about to happen; and, secondly, that the listeners must repent, (change their whole mentality), if they are to benefit from the News. The epiclesis of St Hippolytus asks for *the confirmation of the faith in truth*. Other Eucharistic Prayers expand their list of petitions. The Eucharistic Prayer taken from the *Apostolic Constitutions* first reminds us that the Holy Spirit is the link between our celebration and the sufferings and death of Jesus Christ. After asking for Christ's manifestation, it lists the different dimensions of our relationship with God through the action of the Holy Spirit: that we may be confirmed in piety, receive pardon for our sins, be freed from the devil and his seductions, receive the fullness of the Spirit, may be made worthy of Christ, reach eternal life and be reconciled with the Father. The *Liturgy of St Basil* asks for the gift of unity, and that, rather than suffer condemnation, we will receive mercy and grace together with the saints and especially with the Virgin Mary who, thanks to the Spirit's unifying Power, make up one Church with us. The *Armenian Liturgy of the Katholikos Sahak* prays that the Holy Spirit take up his abode with us, expelling from our minds all suggestions from the devil, and that we should be united in an indissoluble love for our neighbour, and should be saved in soul and body, with pardon for our sins. In another Armenian epiclesis, in the *Anaphora of St Athanasius*, there is a division of labour, the priest praying to the Father according to the Byzantine pattern to send the Spirit, and the choir addressing the Holy Spirit directly to help the souls of the departed:

> Holy Spirit, who descends from heaven and brings about by our hands the Mystery of him with whom you share your glory, by his blood which has been shed, we ask you to give rest to the souls of those among us who have slept.[6]

Perhaps one of the fullest epicleses we have is in the Greek *Liturgy of St James* which, I believe, is only used once a year on St James' feast day. Besides giving a short list of the main events in the Scriptures when the Holy Spirit appears, it includes most of the petitions found in the others:

> Have mercy on us, our God and Saviour. Take pity on us, O God, according to your great mercy, and send on us and on these holy gifts, which we present before you, your most Holy Spirit, Lord and Giver of life, who sits

with You, God our Father, and with your only-begotten Son who reigns with you, consubstantial and co-eternal, who spoke through the Law and the Prophets and descended in the time of the New Covenant in the form of a dove on our Lord Jesus Christ in the River Jordan and remained with him; who descended in the form of tongues of fire on your holy apostles in the Upper Room of holy and glorious Sion on the holy day of Pentecost.

Send, O Lord, this same most Holy Spirit on us and on these holy gifts which we present to you, that he may visit us with his holy, good and glorious presence, and will sanctify them and make this bread the holy body of Christ, and this chalice the precious blood of Christ, so that all those who participate may benefit from the pardon of their sins and receive eternal life, for the sanctification of their souls and bodies, that they may bear good fruit, for the confirmation of the holy, catholic and apostolic Church which you founded on the rock of the faith; that the gates of hell shall not prevail against her, and that she may be liberated by You from all heresy and scandal which come from the workers of iniquity and from those enemies who have risen or who have come to rise against her.[7]

Not all the Eucharistic Prayers asked the Father for the Spirit. The *Anaphora of Serapion*, (fourth century) among possible others, asks the Father to send the *Logos*:

O God of Truth, send down your holy Word on this bread, that the bread may be changed into the body of the Word; and on this chalice, that this chalice may be changed into the blood of the Truth ... [8]

Then there is the Coptic *Anaphora of St Gregory of Nazianzen* which directs the petition for the Holy Spirit, not to the Father, but to Christ:

You, our Lord, transform with your voice these gifts we present before you. You who are here among us, make perfect this liturgy so full of mystery, implant in us the memorial of your holy liturgy; send on to us the grace of your Holy Spirit, so that he will sanctify these gifts which we have placed in your presence, and turn them into the body and blood of our salvation; and make of this bread your body, Lord God and our Saviour, Jesus Christ, handed over for the pardon of sins and eternal life for those who receive it. In the same way, make of this chalice the precious blood of your New Covenant, Lord, God and Saviour, Jesus Christ, handed over for the forgiveness of sins, and eternal life for those who receive it.[9]

This epiclesis brings to mind the 'Pentecost' in St John's Gospel, when the risen Christ appears to his disciples, breaths on them, and says, 'Receive the Holy Spirit' (John 20:19–23). Considering the many facets of the Christian Mystery, how it can be seen from many different angles, and considering the unity of the Blessed Trinity in its activity in creation, we can meditate with profit on these words, and join in with joy with the Copts when they celebrate their Liturgy, while preferring the classical pattern of a prayer to the Father, because it expresses our oneness with Christ in his self-offering to the Father.

The *Roman Canon*, which until Vatican II was the only Eucharistic Prayer in use in the Roman Rite, has an epiclesis for consecration before the words of institution and repeats the request in different and highly significant words after the words of institution and after the memorial of Christ's death, resurrection and ascension, before asking that those who communicate be filled with every blessing. This is not to be wondered at if epiclesis is a characteristic of the whole Eucharistic Prayer. In these prayers there is no mention of the Holy Spirit. I have my own theory why this is. The Roman Canon interprets the Eucharist as an *ascent* of the bread and wine to be made one with Christ in heaven, and an *ascent* into the presence of the Father of the church community by sharing in the memorial of Christ's death, resurrection and ascension, where we share the fellowship of the apostles and martyrs in glorifying him. Hence there is no mention of *descent*, either of the Holy Spirit on the bread and wine or of the Second Coming of Christ. It is all about looking upwards, entering the kingdom of heaven. In accordance with this pattern, the Holy Spirit's role in the consecration of the elements is better expressed in the upward movement of the doxology than in the epiclesis. Here is the first *petition for consecration:*

> Bless and approve our offering; make it acceptable to you, an offering in spirit and in truth. Let it become for us the body and blood of Jesus Christ, your only Son, our Lord.

Here is the *petition* after the words of institution:

> Almighty God, we pray that your angel may take this sacrifice to your altar in heaven. Then, as we receive from this altar the sacred body and blood of your Son, let us be filled with every grace and blessing.

This prayer may well be one of the most ancient in any liturgy in current use, as it reflects the Jewish world at the very beginnings of Christianity and before, in which angels are the contacts between God and human beings (Tobias and, perhaps John 1:51).

The Eucharistic Prayers composed after Vatican II ask simply that those who receive Christ's body and blood be brought together into the unity of the Holy Spirit. However, looking at these fuller prayers, we see that Christian unity exists on many levels. The second Preface of the Holy Eucharist gives us a list of the effects of receiving the Eucharist which parallels the petition of the epiclesis. The priest prays:

With this sacrament you feed and sanctify your faithful, that they may be enlightened by the same faith and that you may bring together by your same love all people who dwell in the same world. Therefore we come together round the table of this wonderful sacrament so that the sheer abundance of your grace may lift us up to possess eternal life. Because of this, Lord, all your creatures in heaven and earth adore you, singing a new song ...

Christian unity begins within our own minds, with the expulsion of evil and divisive thoughts, with the forgiveness of sins which separate us from God, with our protection by the Spirit from the devil whose name signifies *separation*. It brings us into a community which is united by faith and love. The Spirit confirms our faith in truth and allows us to share the same understanding of God's revelation in all places; and he leads us to love God and one another, because he makes us instruments of Christ who becomes our life and our environment where we bask in his love. As our faculty to love is purified by grace, so it becomes universal and embraces the whole human race, and even the whole cosmos, a reflection of God's love. We are called to be – in Mother Teresa's words – missionaries of God's love, crossing every barrier, including the barrier between believers and unbelievers, even the barrier between the living and the dead; and we become intimately united to all whom God loves. As it is our privilege and duty to share the eternal life now, a life that God wishes all human beings to enjoy, we adore and sing the praises of God in the name of all, and in the name of Jesus, Saviour of the world. All this is the work of the Spirit whom we receive from both the Father and the Son in the Mass. The Mass is Pentecost because, as the Holy Spirit came down on the apostles and others, and they became the Church, so the Holy Spirit comes down in the Mass and makes his abode in the Church, transforming it at every level into Christ's body.

Notes

1. Jeremy Driscoll, *Theology at the Eucharistic Table* (Gracewing, 2003).
2. Irenaeus, *Adversus Haereses* III. 24.15 quoted from Olivier Clément, *The Roots of Christian Mysticism* (New City, 1993), p. 96.
3. Irenaeus, *Adversus Haereses* III. 3.2 quoted Clément, *Roots*. p. 119.
4. Jean Corbon, *The Wellspring of Worship* (Paulist Press, New York, 1988).
5. Martin Pindado and J.M. Sanchez Caro, *La Gran Oracion Eucaristica* (1968). Narciso Lorenzo Leal, 'La Epiclesis y la Divinizacion del Hombre', *Nova et Vetera* enero–junio, 2005.
6. As above, Pindado and Caro, p. 271; Leal, p. 43.
7. Ibid.
8. Pindado and Caro, p. 188; Leal, p. 29.
9. Pindado and Caro, pp. 197–8; Leal, p. 31.

Chapter Eight

Sacrifice, our way to God

The word for 'sacrifice' in Hebrew is *korban,* from a word meaning 'to approach' or 'to come close'. 'Do not approach the Lord without a gift,' instructs Sirach (35:6). Taking our human nature, the Word Incarnate approached God the Father as our representative by humble loving obedience. Jesus' acceptance of crucifixion was an expression of his love, a love that went to such lengths on the cross that there was no room for him to love God and have his own agenda at the same time. He was pure love, pure obedience, pure self-giving, which met the pure, infinite love of the Father; and, by this union of loves, divine and human, opening up a way for all human beings to approach and be united to God. Edith Stein (St Teresa Benedicta of the Cross) wrote:

> There was nothing in Christ through his nature and his free decisions that resisted love. He lived every moment of his existence in the boundless surrender to divine love. But in the Incarnation he had taken upon himself the entire burden of mankind's sin, embraced it with his merciful love, and hidden it in his soul. This he did in the *Ecce venio* ('Behold I come') with which he began his earthly life, and specifically renewed in his baptism, and in the *Fiat!* ('Let it be!') of Gethsemane (Luke 22:39). This is how the expiating fire burned in his inmost being, in his entire, lifelong suffering, in the

most intense form in the Garden of Olives and on the cross, because here the sensible joy of the indestructible union ceased, subjecting him totally to the Passion, and allowing this Passion to become the experience of total abandonment by God. In the *Consummatum est*, 'It is finished' (John 19:30) the end of the expiatory fire is announced as the final return into the eternal, undisturbed union of love in the *Pater, in manus tuus commendo spiritum meum* – 'Father, into your hands I commend my spirit.' (Luke 23:46)[1]

In the Passion and death of Christ our sins were consumed by fire. If we accept this in faith, and if we accept the whole Christ in faith-filled surrender, which means, however, that we choose and walk the path of imitation of Christ, then he will lead us 'through his Passion and cross to the glory of his Resurrection'. This is exactly what is experienced in contemplation: passing through the expiatory flames to the bliss of the union of love. This explains its twofold character. It is death and resurrection. After the *Dark Night*, the *Living Flame* shines forth.[2]

Here is a summary of what Fr R. Cantalamessa OFM (Cap), Preacher to the Pontifical Household, said in Lima in an international retreat for priests, given in 2005 under the auspices of the Charismatic Renewal.

Fr Cantalamessa looks at Christ's Passion, dividing it into three stations or moments: a) Jesus in Gethsemane, b) Jesus bound, scourged and crowned before Pilate, and c) the moment when, 'My God, my God, why have you abandoned me?' turns into 'Into your hands I commend my spirit'. His commentary looks beyond the physical suffering and concentrates on the mental and spiritual suffering of Christ.

He says that the text of Isaiah which says 'He bore our sins' needs to be taken quite literally. 'He became sin for us,' is how St Paul puts it (2 Cor. 5:21). Jesus in Gethsemane was experiencing the weight of all the sins of the world from the very beginning: all the cruelty, injustice, impurity, egoism, dishonesty and so on, that has ever been present on earth. He was also experiencing as a human being that separation from God that is a natural consequence of sin, he for whom God was everything. Fr Cantalamessa said that there are times in the Alps when the hot air that comes from Africa meets the cold air that comes from the North. This shock of hot with cold produces storms, with thunder and lightning. In the Passion, the cold air of sin meets head on the hot winds of God's love; and, through the fidelity of Jesus while suffering the full consequences of sin's evil, sin loses its effect, no longer able to separate us sinners from the love of God.

Jesus' approach to the Father through death to resurrection becomes our own means of approaching the Father, our sacrifice. In the Letter to the Ephesians it is written, 'This was according to the eternal purpose which he has realized in Jesus Christ our Lord in whom we have boldness and confidence of access through our faith in him.' As Jesus is the means by which we approach God with boldness and confidence, he is the sacrifice 'that the Lord has provided' (Gen. 22:8ff). In the Eucharist, we offer the *memorial* of Christ's death and resurrection to the Father; and, because he suffered these things as our representative, and because the same Spirit is contemporaneous with him on the cross and with us at Mass, Christ's sacrifice becomes our sacrifice. His perfect self-surrender gives value to ours, his perfect love embraces ours, his perfect adoration becomes ours. In the words of St Leo the Great:

> Our participation in the Body and Blood of Christ does nothing else except this: that we pass over into what we have received, into Christ; for we have died with Him and have been buried with Him and have been raised

together with Him. And thus we bear Him within, both in our spirit and in our flesh, at all times . . .[3]

All this happens only in so far as we follow in his footsteps, even if we do so hesitatingly and weakly. In order to participate authentically in the Mass, we not only have to take part in the outward ceremony, we also need to inwardly die and rise with Christ. 'Everyone to whom much is given, of him much will be required' (Luke 12:48). As the Holy Spirit forms us more and more in his image, so our internal disposition becomes more in tune with the words we use, and we participate more and more in the Mass. Indeed, as the Mass in any one place is always an act of the whole Church, all Christians participate in it to the degree that they share the life of Christ in the Church they enter at Baptism. The way of the Mass is the way of the cross. St Rose of Lima gives us this prophetic message:

> The Lord raised his voice with incomparable majesty: Let everyone understand that grace comes out of tribulation. You must know that without afflictions you will not reach the heights of grace. Learn that the measure of charisms that you receive will grow the more you work. Let no one deceive himself, this is the only true path to Paradise, and that apart from the cross there is no other way that one can ascend to heaven.[4]

In the Gospel, resurrection and cross are inseparable. We need to take up our own cross and follow in Christ's footsteps. We must have that mind which was in Christ when he humbled himself even to the death of the cross (Phil. 2:5f.). We must bear Christ's death in our bodies so that his life may also reign there (2 Cor. 4:10–11). For this we have been baptized into his death and resurrection (Rom. 6:3f.) which is the rhythm of his body on earth.

Edith Stein writes:

It is one thing to be satisfied with ourselves, being 'good Catholics' who 'fulfil our duties', who read 'good literature' and 'vote as we should' but who follow our own will and desires, and another thing to live in the hands of God with the simplicity of a child and the humility of the publican. He who starts off on this road does not look back. This is what it means to be sons of God, to make oneself small and, at the same time, to make oneself great. To live eucharistically means to leave behind the narrow horizons of one's own life and to adopt the infinite horizons of Christ. He who seeks the Lord in his house does not speak to him merely of himself and his own preoccupations. He will begin to interest himself in the preoccupations of the Lord. The daily participation in the Eucharistic Sacrifice places us, even without us noticing, in the great current of liturgical life.[5]

If a liturgy encourages and expresses this process of identification with Christ in his death and resurrection, and identification with the Church as the body of Christ, then it is a good liturgy, whatever way the priest is facing, whatever language it is in, and whatever the degree of external participation by the people; though, of course, there must always be *some* degree of external participation because it is the nature of liturgy to express outwardly and socially what the Spirit is doing inwardly in the Church. There are many ways that Mass is celebrated in the Catholic Church, and there are many liturgical traditions; but in all of them, our outward communal participation will be the expression of our sharing together as one body in the death and resurrection of Christ in the presence of the Father.

Sharing together in the death and resurrection of Christ makes us a community that is very special indeed, and we should be careful not to be satisfied with anything less. Of this Jesus spoke:

As you, Father, are in me and I in you, may they also be in us, so that the world may believe that you have sent me. The glory that you have given me I have given them, so that they may be one, as we are one, I in them and you in me, that they may become completely one, so that the world may know that you have sent me and have loved them even as you have loved me. (John 17:21–3)

We must remember that, in St John's Gospel, Jesus was 'glorified' on the cross when he manifested his obedient love 'unto death'. He revealed to us that 'God is Love'. This 'glory' that Jesus manifested in his solitary death is manifested in the Church through its communal life. A community of this kind, based as it is on self-giving, has 'one heart and one soul'. This involves sharing in Christ's death in order to enjoy a new communal life in God, a life that reflects and reveals to the world something of the Blessed Trinity: a necessary prerequisite for the conversion of the world.

In the Mass, the Church becomes the sacrament of Christ 'because we pass over into him whom we receive' (St Leo the Great). Because of our *communion* with Christ and our being part of the modern world, we are the sacrament of Christ among our contemporaries. The Mass is *sacrifice*; and, as we make our own his death and resurrection, we pass through the veil of his body and blood into the presence of the Father. Because of this we become the sacrament of him who is the *acceptable face of humanity* in the depths of the Blessed Trinity. In that role we offer the prayers and good deeds and religious and human activity, not only of ourselves but of the whole race, to the Father in Christ's name, giving to all these activities a value for salvation they would never have without the celebration of the Eucharist. The Mass is *proclamation*. It begins with the proclamation of the Word in the readings and their explanation according to the mind of the Church in the sermon; but this proclamation reaches its climax when the Word is made flesh at the consecration and we receive Christ himself in communion. 'When we eat this bread and drink this cup, we proclaim your death, Lord Jesus, until you come in glory.' We are then sent forth to carry Christ's message to the world. We become the sacrament of Christ, the *human face of God*, made visible to the world by our words and, even more, by the quality of our love. The purer this love becomes, the more Christlike we become, the more our love becomes an instrument of Christ's own love for the whole of humankind, and even for the whole universe. Père Spicq OP, Professor of New Testament at Fribourg where I studied theology, used to say, commenting on John 17:21, that, as far as the world is concerned, the Church is only visible by its love, and renders itself invisible by its lack of love.

There are *ecclesial communities* which separated themselves from the Catholic Church at the Reformation and, because of the particular nature of their heresy, became distinct bodies without apostolic succession, even though they are communities of authentic Christian faith and practice. According to Vatican II, these 'communities, though we believe they suffer from defects ... have by no means been deprived of significance and importance in the mystery of salvation. For the Spirit of Christ has not refrained from using them as means of salvation which derive their efficacy from the very fullness of grace and truth entrusted to the Catholic Church'.[6] The Holy Spirit uses those things that these communities have in common with the Catholic Church to make them a means of grace. However, what can be said of their Holy Communion services? – which the Church regards as invalid, partly because of a lack of apostolic succession and partly because it regards their teaching on the Eucharist to be gravely deficient. We must remember that, however deficient their understanding of the Eucharist may be, they are attempting to fulfil Christ's command to 'do this in remembrance of me' and they do believe that they are having some kind of communion with Christ. Often there are other similarities, especially when they have been influenced by the liturgical movement, and many are closer to the Catholic Church on the Eucharist because of changes and a movement of convergence in all our churches. Nevertheless, these changes are not universal, and there still remains the problem of apostolic succession. The question can be put: because of the vestiges of Catholicism in their Eucharistic services, are they a means of grace, or is grace received merely due to the subjective dispositions of the participants? In itself, is their ritual an empty shell? The pastoral practice of the Catholic Church seems inconsistent here. On the one hand it considers these Protestant Eucharists as invalid; on the other hand, they will allow a Protestant to take communion in the Catholic Church if he believes in the Real Presence and is unable to go to communion in his own church for some considerable time. If the Protestant Eucharist is simply invalid, how can someone suffer spiritually by being deprived of it?

If the Catholic Eucharist includes in its scope all the prayers and good deeds expressed in religious and ordinary human activity of the whole human race, and gives them a value they would not have without the celebration of Mass, *a fortiori* this would include the Eucharistic services of communities who celebrate in good faith, but without apostolic succession. This would mean that Protestant communion services receive from the Catholic Mass a value they would not have without it, because the Holy Spirit who is invoked on the Church at the Catholic Eucharist includes them too. Of course, this benefit to them is the work of the Holy Spirit and does not depend on us, while the same Spirit ensures that their communion with us, though imperfect, contributes to the good of the whole body, including us who are members of the Catholic Church.

Hence the Catholic Church fulfils itself as body of Christ in the world by embracing by the power of the

Holy Spirit the whole of human activity, everything that can be offered to God, hence everything except sin, and offers it up to God in the Mass, including it in Christ's sacrifice. In this way, everything is sanctified because 'all life, all holiness comes from the Father through Jesus Christ, by the work of the Holy Spirit', and 'All honour and glory' from whatever source is offered to the Father 'through him, with him and in him in the unity of the Holy Spirit'. Just as the Holy Spirit united Christ with the whole human race in his sacrifice on the cross, so the same Spirit unites the whole human race to what we are doing when we celebrate the Eucharist. For this reason, Bishop Christopher Butler said after Vatican II, 'Before the Council, I knew where the Church was and I knew where it wasn't; now I still know where it is, but I no longer know where it isn't.'

It is due to the Mass and the love of God that flows from it onto the human race like the river of fire that flows from the throne of God (Dan. 7:10), that we can call Catholicism truly universal: it embraces the universe. About the universality of Catholicism de Lubac wrote:

> [The Catholic Church is] neither Latin nor Greek, but universal ... Nothing authentically human, whatever its origin, can be alien to her ... In her, man's desires and God's have their meeting-place, and by teaching all men their obligations she wishes at the same time to satisfy and more than satisfy the yearnings of each soul and of every age; to gather in everything for its salvation and sanctification ... To see in Catholicism one religion among others ... even if it be added that it is the only true religion, the only system that works, is to mistake its very nature, or at least to stop at the threshold. Catholicism is religion itself. It is the form that humanity must put on in order finally to be itself. It is the only reality which involves by its existence no opposition. It is therefore the very opposite of a 'closed society'.[7]

Thanks to our understanding of the Mass, we see all religion and human activity now in the context of 'the love of God, the grace of Our Lord Jesus Christ and the fellowship of the Holy Spirit'; so we can be relaxed about it. As Fr Paul McPartlan wrote,[8] we must argue less and love more, because our religion is about the love of God for the whole of humankind and for the whole universe. Whenever we cease to love people, even when our arguments are devastating and watertight, we make God's kingdom invisible to their gaze. We think the problem is them, but it is ourselves.

Notes

1. See above, ch. 3, n. 1.
2. Ibid.
3. St Leo the Great, *Sermo* 63:7, 135–141, *CCSL* 138A, p. 38.
4. Letter 'Al medico Castillo' in L. Getino OP (ed.), *Santa Rosa de Lima, La Patrona de América* (Madrid, 1928), pp. 54–5.
5. See above ch. 3, n. 1.
6. Decree on Ecumenism ch. 1.3. *The Documents of Vatican II* (Geoffrey Chapman, London and Dublin, 1966), p. 346.
7. Henri de Lubac, *Catholicism* (Universe Books, Burns & Oates, 1962).
8. Paul McPartlan, 'The Idea of the Church: Abbot Butler and Vatican II', *Downside Review* (January 2003).

Chapter Nine

The Mass and the martyrs

In the primitive Church, the Mass was linked to martyrdom. This is clear in the eye-witness account of the martyrdom of St Polycarp, bishop of Smyrna. He was condemned to be burnt alive because he refused to recognize the divinity of the emperor. He asked his executioners not to nail him to the stake because the same Lord who gave him strength to brave the flames would also give him courage to remain in them without moving:

> As the very best ram chosen from the flock for sacrifice, a holocaust pleasing to God, lifting his eyes to heaven, he said, 'Lord God Almighty, Father of your beloved and blessed Son, Jesus Christ, through whom we have come to know you, God of the angels, of the powers and of all creation, and of all your holy people who live in your sight. I bless you because you have been pleased to give me this day and hour as a gift, so that I may be able to participate with your martyrs in the chalice of your Christ and to rise to eternal life in body and soul through the immortality of the Holy Spirit. May I be received today with them in your presence as a rich and acceptable sacrifice, O true and infallible God, as you prepared and revealed it beforehand and have now accomplished. I praise you for everything. I bless and glorify you through the eternal and heavenly high priest Jesus Christ, your beloved Son, through

whom may you and the Holy Spirit receive glory now and for ages to come. Amen.[1]

It is highly probable that this is a Eucharistic prayer that has been adapted to the occasion. Certainly it has the ingredients of a Eucharistic prayer: thanksgiving and praise for past events and for the present occasion, reference to the transforming power of the Holy Spirit who, in this case, was to make him immortal, a number of petitions, finishing with a doxology. Jesus is depicted both as the means by which we know the Father and the means by which Polycarp's prayer and, indeed, all glory is rendered to the Father. The bishop mentions participating with the martyrs in the 'chalice of your Christ' in the same sentence as he speaks of the Holy Spirit. In the early Church, the gift of the Holy Spirit was specially linked with the reception of the chalice because, among the Jews and, I think, the Stoics, the spirit of anybody was considered to be contained in the blood. Because of what later came to be called the Incarnation, the blood of Christ was considered to be the vehicle of the Holy Spirit. Hence a homily inspired by St Hippolytus says:

> We are fed with the bread from heaven; our thirst is quenched by the cup of joy, the chalice afire with the Spirit, the blood wholly warmed from on high by the Spirit.[2]

St Ambrose of Milan echoes the same tradition:

> Every time you drink, you receive the forgiveness of your sins and you are intoxicated with the Spirit. That is why the Apostle said, 'Be not drunk with wine, but be filled with the Spirit'. For one who is drunk with wine totters and reels. But one who is intoxicated with the Spirit is rooted in Christ.[3]

If this is so, then the cup of suffering which Jesus asked

should pass from him in the garden of Gethsemane, which he asked his disciples if they were ready to partake, and in which the martyrs shared, is associated with the cup at Mass. There is a further Eucharistic reference in the account: as the flames leapt up, St Polycarp's body did not look like flesh, but rather like freshly-baked bread.

Another Father who sees his martyrdom in terms of the Eucharist is St Ignatius of Antioch. He is being taken in chains to Rome, and he writes ahead to the church there, begging them not to use their influence to rescue him from martyrdom because he longs to die for Christ. He writes,

> Permit me to be food for the wild beasts through which I can arrive before God. I am God's wheat and will be milled by the teeth of the beasts that I may become Christ's pure bread ... Pray to Christ for me that through these instruments [the beasts] I may be a sacrifice for God.[4]

We become what we eat. As it says in the *Didache*, just as grains of wheat are gathered from far and wide to become one single loaf, losing their individuality but fulfilling their destiny, so we come from different places to the Eucharist and, baked together by the fire of the Holy Spirit to become one single loaf which is the body of Christ, we lose our false individuality and autonomy, but fulfil the purpose for which we were created in an intimate union with Christ in his sacrifice, thus entering the kingdom of God. For St Ignatius, what he would do in the arena was simply a logical consequence following on from what he celebrated in the Mass.

Ignatius saw a parallel between Christ giving himself to be our food and drink, (this self-surrender being an expression of Christ's sacrifice to the Father), and that of himself, giving himself to the beasts and thus becoming a sacrifice, 'Christ's pure bread'. For Ignatius and Polycarp, there are three moments of sacrifice, Jesus on the cross,

Jesus and the Church in the Eucharist, and their own martyrdom; and all three are intimately connected. In his passion, Jesus offered himself to the Father by putting himself at the disposition of the Jewish authorities and accepting patiently the consequences. In the Mass, Jesus expresses his self-offering to the Father by putting himself at our disposition as food and drink. Through communion in his sacrifice, the martyr identifies himself with Christ and offers himself to the Father by putting himself at the disposition of the Roman authorities and fully accepting the consequences, becoming 'Christ's pure bread'.

When we as the Church take part in the Mass and receive Christ in communion, we associate ourselves with his self-offering, receiving the Holy Spirit who is the Son's act of self-giving to the Father as well as the Father's act of self-giving to the Son, and expressing our willingness to give all and to receive all with Him. Like Jesus, we become 'an everlasting gift' to the Father (Eucharistic Prayer III), 'a living sacrifice of praise' (Eucharistic Prayer IV). It is clear to Polycarp and all the martyrs that receiving the chalice at Mass may well lead to accepting the cup of suffering in martyrdom, because, in both, we offer the same gift of ourselves in Christ to the Father. Through our participation in the Mass we become spiritually martyrs, witnessing to the world the reality of Christ by our self-giving. Thus Catholic spirituality has the same effect, however different it may seem in form, as that of Orthodox spirituality. In the words of Paul Evdokimov:

> Every special 'method' in Orthodoxy consists in making the mind descend into the heart to awaken there, by the invocation of the name of Jesus, his Eucharistic presence. So 'ground by the millstone of humility', man becomes 'a bread acceptable to the Lord' in the likeness of the martyr who, 'ground by the teeth of the beasts', is transformed, by the grace of the Cross, into the definitive Eucharist.[5]

It is interesting that the first texts which describe St Peter's association with the church in Rome do not say that he was the first bishop. For St Irenaeus, for example, what is significant is that Saints Peter and Paul were apostles, founders of the Roman Church, and were martyred there. I would suggest that a martyr was considered to be united to the Eucharistic community by a much more permanent and strong bond even than the bishop, especially when the Eucharist was celebrated over the very spot where he or she had been buried. Being the bishop of a local church belongs to the external celebration of the Eucharist in that church which is temporary: martyrs belong to that dimension of the Eucharist and of the Church which is the same in every celebration. Bishops come and go by the very nature of things; though, of course, the Episcopal College belongs to the permanent structure of the Church. Martyrs, on the other hand, pass from time into eternity; and, as the Eucharist embraces heaven and earth, they become permanent members of the Eucharistic community. Hence the writers of the Roman Canon are very conscious that they celebrate the Mass in fellowship with the apostles and martyrs. It is the martyr's unity in the very substance of the sacrifice of Christ that makes him one with the very substance of the Church down the ages. From this we learn that, while our external participation in the Mass is in itself an ephemeral event, by making his sacrifice our own, by becoming, in the words of St Ignatius, 'Christ's pure bread', we touch eternity and become with the martyrs participants in the 'definitive Eucharist' in heaven.

A martyr was a witness to the pagan world, but even more a witness to fellow members of the Church, because they did externally what all who take part in the Mass should do interiorly: they offered their whole selves to God in union with Christ on the cross. This is why we can never separate liturgy from spirituality. We can only offer ourselves to the Father, and hence become one with the Son, to the degree that we are transformed by the Holy

Spirit; and this we pray for at the epiclesis. At our human level, it is a process which, elsewhere, I have described in terms of living the Beatitudes. Someone who is transformed by the Spirit receives the divine life from the Father because he is 'in' the Son. This process progresses to the degree that he has attained *purity of heart* through ever-deepening humility and love. This means that he is ever more identified with Christ in his sacrifice, more at one with the Eucharist. He thus becomes a source of salvation for others – what in the Beatitudes is called a *peacemaker* – because his very being is transformed by the Spirit of the risen Christ, and this union with Christ makes him truly a son of God. St Gregory Palamas wrote that this *theosis* or deification is not just an individual thing: it becomes a privileged means by which God manifests himself to the world. He wrote, 'The Saints participate in God. They not only participate, but they communicate him ... They not only live, but also bring to life, and that is not the attribute of a created faculty.' He writes of the divine light that it is 'a gift of deification ... a gift of the Holy Spirit, a grace by which God alone shines through the intermediary of the soul and body of those who are truly worthy of this'.[6]

To the degree of our own self-giving to the Father, we are transformed from within by the divine life, and we are able to offer our transformed humanity to the world in humble service. Dying with Christ in order to rise with him is what Christianity is all about, what the Mass is about, and what martyrs illustrate by their deaths. Hence, receiving communion is a challenge to let others share our humanity as we share in that of Christ; and this involves dying to self and hence allowing ourselves to be transformed by the Spirit, offering ourselves with Christ to the Father and, by so doing, following in the steps of the martyrs and becoming part of what is eternal in the Church.

Notes

1. *The Martyrdom of Polycarp*, SC 10.242.
2. An anonymous *Homily* inspired by Hippolytus, *Treatise on Easter*, Exordium 8 (*SC* 27, pp. 133, 135), quoted from Olivier Clément, *The Roots of Christian Mysticism*, p. 113.
3. Ambrose of Milan, *The Sacraments* V.13, 17 (*SC* 25, p. 92) quoted from Clément, *Roots*, p. 114.
4. Ignatius of Antioch, *To the Romans*, 4–7 (*SC* 10, p. 130).
5. Paul Evdokimov, 'Spiritualité orthodoxe et vie spirituelle dans l'Orthodoxie' in *L'Unité Chrétienne* xx, November 1970, p. 24.
6. Quoted from John Meyendorff, *A Study of Gregory Palamas* (Faith Press, 1964).

Part Two
Practice

Chapter Ten

Celebrating

In the student circles in which I moved after the Vatican Council it was commonly believed that the reformed Mass had two main characteristics. We believed that the primary purpose of the Mass is to mould a group of people into the body of Christ which, in turn, would go out into the world and do Christlike things in his name. The second characteristic flowed from the first: accent was placed on the personal relationships of those taking part, and, at least in student circles, much stress was laid on warm feelings and informality as signs that we were on the Vatican II wavelength. However, we saw in the first part of the book that, according to the constitution *Sacrosanctum Concilium* and reflected in the Eucharistic prayers, the liturgy is a *theophany*, a manifestation of God's saving presence in Christ; and we are not only brought into his presence like Moses; we are taken up into the very life of the Trinity by our communion with Christ, and then we manifest his presence to the world through our Christian lives.

    Rowan Williams, in his book *The Dwelling of the Light*,[1] has a beautiful meditation on the icon by A. Rublev called 'The Hospitality of Abraham' which depicts the three angels at a table on which there is food. The angels stand for the Blessed Trinity and the food suggests the Eucharist. The angel who represents the Son points towards it in a gesture of blessing. The Christian who is contemplating the icon is the invisible fourth person at the table, sharing in the life of the Trinity by partaking in the Eucharist.

If we want to know what kind of attitude is appropriate in the presence of such a manifestation of God's Presence, we can imagine Moses and the people standing before the Tent of Meeting. Moses represented the people before God and represented God before the people: but he, no less than they, was entering into the divine Presence. He was not the centre of attention. So it is with the priest in the Mass. The secret of celebrating Mass fittingly is for the priest to represent Christ without getting in his way or, even worse, replacing him as the centre of attention. Priest and people are closer to God than were Moses and the People of Israel before the Tent of Meeting, because we are admitted into God to share his very life in a way only made possible by the Incarnation. We must take our cue from Isaiah 6, and from the author of the Book of Revelation: both showed, not so much human warmth and informality in the Presence of God, but – in the words from the Letter to the Hebrews – *reverence* and *awe*. There is plenty of evidence from the Fathers and from the wording of the liturgy that this is the traditional approach. He who loses a sense of the divine Presence at Mass loses a sense of what the Mass is about.

We looked for human warmth and informality but should have been looking for reverence and awe. When reverence and awe are lost, our sense of God's presence and the corresponding sense of sin also disappear. The next thing we do is lapse from the faith. We have watched it happen. However, were we not right to expect warmth and, where appropriate and possible, informality, to be special signs of the spirit of Vatican II? Was not John XXIII the most informal of men? Is not human warmth a characteristic of every properly-functioning community where love reigns supreme? Is it not what every potential recruit for the monastic life looks for when he or she visits a monastery, even when it is a community totally dedicated to seeking God? Apart from the accusation of infidelity, is not the worst possible criticism of a Christian family or a religious community that it is cold, where every member lives each for him or herself? If all this is so, should not this warmth be evident, even in the celebration of the liturgy?

The short answer is 'Yes' to all these questions. Our error was to confuse the fruit of a good liturgy with the way it is to be performed. The warmth that characterizes Christian community is the fruit of much sacrifice, not the sacrifice itself. Only a person who can say 'no' to himself can say 'yes' to God and to others in a way that does not depend on his likes or dislikes, his temperament, his moods, his convenience or self-interest. In the Eucharist, we become one with Christ on the cross, and out of this sacrifice come communion, warmth, oneness, fraternal love by the bucketful; but what we do in the Mass is seek God with reverence and awe. May I suggest to the readers a little experiment? Let them seek out the strictest monastery of men or women they can find. If possible, let them meet the community. I would be prepared to bet that, all things being equal, they will not find a happier or more united group of people anywhere. Let them go to a hospital in Lourdes where all the doctors and nurses are sacrificing their holiday to serve the sick and who even pay for the privilege, and they will find all the human warmth and happiness they want. It is the same both in Christian marriage and religious life: we can only find fulfilment in communion when we put aside our egotism and put God and others first. He who loses his life shall save it: that is the way of the cross, of the Mass and of the Christian life. To turn the Mass primarily into a means of celebrating human warmth and togetherness can lead us to a bogus resurrection without the cross; but when a group of people truly put themselves in God's hands, saying with Jesus, 'Not my will but yours be done', then human warmth will invade the liturgy, however it is celebrated.

Liturgy is a drama by which the participants are led through symbolic word and action into the presence of God who is the principal actor, even though invisible. We who are preparing to celebrate the liturgy must ask ourselves what kind of ritual will help priest and people to become aware of God's presence and to accept through their participation his gift of divine life. Reverence and awe will follow awareness. The words of the liturgy are clear enough; but how are we going to help people become aware of the fact that, when we pray and sing, we are sharing in Christ's prayer; when the word is proclaimed, Christ is speaking to us; that the priest, who is our voice, when he prays the Eucharistic prayer, is uttering Christ's prayer as well as our own? How are we going to make them aware that Christ's prayer which we summarize in the words, 'This is my body ... This is my blood', implies a total gift of himself to the Father and to us, and that, in offering him to the Father as our representative, we are also offering ourselves, and that the level of our subsequent communion depends on how real is our gift of ourselves to him? How are we going to make people aware of the fact that, by participation in the Mass, we are participating, with the angels and saints, in the life of the Blessed Trinity? These are the real questions about how to celebrate the Mass, and they are based on the teaching of Vatican II. Answer these and respond to the challenge, and there will be no need to worry about the love of Christians for each other: the Mass will be awash with it. Unless the vision of Christ's continuous presence can be glimpsed in and through the ceremonial of the Mass, these truths will remain abstract and unconnected with peoples' daily lives, and the whole purpose of liturgical reform will be frustrated.

There is nothing wrong with the text of the post-Vatican II Mass. The Eucharistic prayers are based on the very best models and express the breadth of the Catholic liturgical tradition in a way never equalled before. For this very reason, the stress of these prayers is on the vertical relationship between the community and God. This is at variance with much of the liturgical practice since the council which has stressed the horizontal relationships between priest and people. It has led to a rather absurd situation where words clearly spoken to God in the text are spoken by the priest as though he is addressing the people. Too often, the priest seems mainly conscious of the presence of the people, and the people mainly conscious of the presence of the priest, but it is God whom priest and people alike have come to meet through sacrifice in the Mass.

In other words, 'Mass facing the people' can cause as many problems as it solves. The very term reflects a pre-Vatican II outlook and a reaction to it by people who still think in the same categories, where the 'Mass' is what the priest does in front of the people, instead of what priest and people do together, with different functions but the same Spirit. In Vatican II and in the patristic tradition, Christ is present throughout the Mass in various ways and degrees of intensity and acts through readers and through the congregation when it prays and sings, as well as through the priest, making the Mass a communal act, a harmonious whole. The phrase 'Mass with his back to the people' also misrepresents the other practice where what is significant is not the back of the priest but the fact that the whole community, priest and people, are facing in the same direction. Although stressing the communal dimension of the Mass, the newer practice might be interpreted as the epitome of clericalism, because the priest can become the focus of attention in an unprecedented manner.

On the other hand, I am not advocating a reversal of the newer practice either. I have been present at many a Mass which has been devoutly, fittingly and even wonderfully celebrated. There are problems with both ways of celebrating the Eucharist, and, perhaps, with any way that could be devised: the problem is people. Perhaps what I am suggesting is that it is possible to have a very fine liturgy with the priest facing East, as long as the people are in agreement and the Mass retains its communal character, and the same can be said of liturgies where the priest faces the people, as long as he directs the prayer toward God and does not turn the liturgy into a rather odd class of religious instruction. Byzantine Christians will continue to worship with the altar facing East; and we shall continue to face the people, except for those who adhere to the earlier liturgical tradition. Both positions stand for something important and should complement each other. I think we should forget the 'conservative' and 'progressive' paradigm which we have inherited from Vatican II times: they are neither theological nor liturgical words, having been borrowed from politics, and tend to warp serious discussion and discourage profound thought.

If we want reverence and awe, we must start with ourselves through prayer and meditation, and then with the people who are most involved in the liturgy, the priests, the altar servers, the readers and the Eucharistic ministers. In saying this, I am, perhaps, influenced by the fact that most of my parish experience has been in Peru. The numbers are too great to have a personal relationship with the whole parish. We concentrate on training our pastoral teams and getting to know them very well. It is important that readers should understand the privilege, the responsibility and the level of commitment required to lend our lips to God as readers. Let them read of parallel situations in the Old and New Testaments. I know of a parish in Mexico where people are not just asked to read on the spur of the moment, without preparation. The readers are prepared for their office by prayer and instruction. Much is made of choosing them. Like Moses on Mount Sinai and the prophet in chapter 6 of Isaiah, the reader is brought into the presence of God and charged with giving God's word to the people. Hence, in this Mexican parish, they are advised to go to confession before starting their stint of reading because, just like Isaiah, they are people of unclean lips. The Eucharistic ministers in the parish are chosen from among those who have served the community the longest and are most regular in their Christian lives. When a young Mexican who attends a British university was asked by his chaplain to be a Eucharistic minister, he was filled with awe and asked me if he could accept. The training in Mexico had obviously worked.

Another step in the right direction is to treat the ambo with respect and reverence. The ambo should only be used for reading the Word of God and for praying to God: it is a sacred place, and is not for notices or a place from which to direct the choir. One of the differences of emphasis between Catholicism and classical Reformed Protestantism is that, for Catholics, the Word is primarily the spoken Word: Christ speaks in the liturgical readings, is interpreted within the context of Catholic liturgical tradition and 'becomes flesh' in the Eucharist; while, for Protestants, it is primarily a written text and stands on its own. The ambo is the place from which Christ speaks, using the reader as his instrument. Reserving it for that function will help the reader to appreciate what is happening when he fulfils his office, and this appreciation may even reach the people.

As anyone will notice who goes into a modern church inspired by the contemporary liturgy – in Liverpool or Clifton Cathedrals, for example – the sanctuary, as such, is not emphasized. In the reformed rite it is not the holiest part of the Church, the place where God is imagined to be: it has become a stage which allows all who take part to have visual contact with the altar. Even in traditional buildings, once the altar faces the people, the sanctuary tends to lose its sacred character and becomes a stage. According to the insights of Vatican II, the whole church is a sanctuary because it houses the body of Christ, the Church. Simply as Christians, 'we have confidence to enter the sanctuary by the blood of Jesus, by the new and living way that he opened for us through the curtain (that is, through his flesh), and since we have a great priest over the house of God, let us approach with a true heart in full assurance of faith, with our hearts sprinkled clean from an evil conscience and our bodies washed with pure water ' (Heb. 10:19–22). Having been cleansed in soul and body by baptism, we enter the heavenly sanctuary into the Presence of the Father through the veil which is Christ's flesh, through communion. Thus, in the liturgy, as it has developed since Vatican II, the altar is the central symbol of God's presence for priest and people alike, the main place where God acts. It is the Gate of Christ between heaven and earth, representing the altar in heaven (Eucharistic Prayer I), the symbol among us of the Eucharistic heart of Christ, as Nicholas Cabasilas put it. St John Chrysostom writes:

> When the priest stands before the holy table and, with hands extended towards heaven, asks the Holy Spirit to come and touch the offered gifts, a great calm, a profound silence is necessary: when the Spirit grants his grace, when he touches the offerings, and when you see the lamb immolated and consumed. I imagine Elias, surrounded by a huge crowd, the victim stretched out on the stones, everyone enveloped in silence and quiet, and only the prophet praying; and suddenly, a flame descends from heaven onto the sacrifice ... The priest [in the Eucharist] is standing, not so that a mere flame should descend, but the Holy Spirit.

('Lamb' is the name given in Byzantine Christianity to what we call the 'host', which is immolated and consumed by becoming the acceptable sacrifice, the body of Christ.)

The altar should be, quite obviously, the most important piece of furniture in the church, the place to which all eyes are drawn. If possible, it should be imposing. After all, God is going to use it. The trouble is that, owing to a defective theology, priests can be more conscious of their 'power to consecrate' given them at ordination, than they are of God's present activity in the Mass through the Spirit. The new emphasis on the epiclesis should rectify this in time. Another problem is that, quite often, there is an imposing but dead altar gathering dust against the east wall of the sanctuary, while the altar in use looks more like a card table in comparison. Often the old altar is still there because the people are attached to it, or because it has great artistic merit, or because the church cannot be imagined without it. In these cases, it would seem to me sensible and correct to *use* the old altar rather than a far less imposing, and often quite makeshift affair currently in use. There are real benefits to be gained in facing east. A very simple principle can be used: that the priest faces east when he is speaking to God, and faces the people when he is speaking to them. In this way there is no confusion as to whom he is speaking. Microphones can do the rest.

Some horrible things have happened in the name of liturgical reform. Recently, I visited two churches in Peru that are in the hands of the Neo-catechumenate. One was purpose-built, while the other was a traditional, Spanish-type church. They had an identical lay-out: the priest's chair, then the ambo for reading the Word, then a large square altar, and then the baptismal font. The chair of the celebrant represents the head of the body, the ambo represents the mouth, the altar represents the stomach, and the baptismal font represents the womb. The people sit round this central space, most of them down the main sides of the church, as though in choir stalls, and, together with the priest, constitute the body of Christ. I was impressed by the modern church which, though breaking with tradition in some ways, does so in a theologically and liturgically coherent way. Its font was of a kind that you descend into using steps. The same arrangement in the other church which was built for another kind of liturgy was very ugly indeed.

At the Reformation, people did nasty things to the cathedrals and parish churches throughout England.

They became dominated by over-large pulpits in the wrong place, while communion tables replaced altars. But these churches and cathedrals were Catholic churches, built by Catholics for Catholics; and, quietly but persistently, the stones whispered Catholicism to the people who used them, while the preachers shouted Protestantism from the pulpit. Then, one day, people listened to the building, and began to replace the communion tables with altars, and the pulpits shrank and went back to where they belong, and the priests put on vestments. Church buildings cannot help but express the vision of those who built them, and, although their voices are muted, they are too big and too permanent to contradict for ever. One day, the less felicitous changes after Vatican II will be undone. I am certain that it is good liturgical sense to make use of the setting in which the Mass is celebrated, rather than ignore it or, even worse, to act in spite of it.

Another important factor in the liturgy is the music. Inappropriate music can hide what is happening very successfully. It is possible to participate in everything and to miss the whole point of what is said and done, simply because the music expresses a different mood from the words. Good music can be conducive to prayer, while bad music can only entertain. Moreover, good music can help us to listen, as can the intelligent use of silence. Good liturgy will engage our whole being, to the very depths of the soul. We need to interiorize the Mass, even as we participate exteriorly in the celebration, so that we can realize what is taking place and, to a certain extent, experience and savour what God is doing in our midst.

Note
1. Rowan Williams, *The Dwelling of the Light: Praying with Icons of Christ* (Canterbury Press, 2003).

Chapter Eleven

Variety in Unity

In 2005, I was invited to participate in the Easter Liturgy in the Greek Catholic Ukrainian parish in Gloucester, and it was a moving experience. Many years before, I went to Chevetogne for Holy Week. Chevetogne is a Benedictine monastery in Belgium where the Byzantine Liturgy is celebrated according to the Russian use. The liturgy in Chevetogne is celebrated perfectly, but this was the first time I was to take part in a parish celebration. It was even more authentic because a number of people had come from the Ukraine to celebrate Easter with their relatives in England. Several made the point in conversation afterwards that they had no written music: everything was known by heart and had been passed down from generation to generation. The gusto with which they sang, the joy on their faces, the expectant way they looked at each other every time they began a new liturgical song, all contributed to a celebration which was as ceremonious as a papal Mass and as spontaneous as a charismatic prayer meeting; and the spontaneity came from deep down within them. It showed that they were part of the liturgy, and the liturgy was an essential part of them.

I knew that we would never have that kind of relationship with the liturgy in the West, at least in this century. It is not something taught in school, but ingested with their mothers' milk. It is not something they plan: it has grown organically as part of their culture. To develop that kind of liturgy we would need a traditional society, and ours is a society of novelty, with only the barest threads of tradition. If we cannot have this kind of liturgy, what is open to us? What is God offering us?

The first thing I have learned about our modern liturgy is the more that those who celebrate it are involved in its preparation, the more effective it is. There is much opportunity for such co-operation between priest and people in the post-Vatican II Mass, and we should make use of it. If we cannot have a liturgy that is ours because it is part of our very culture like the Ukrainians, we can have a liturgy we make our own by helping to prepare it. This means that training in the liturgy must be a part of the ordinary Christian's formation.

The second characteristic of the modern liturgy follows from the first: there is a considerable variety in the ways that Mass is celebrated, a variety that is only limited by the nature of the Eucharist and the words and structure of the rite. Imagine a city where there are several Eastern Catholic parishes for immigrants, Neo-Catechumenate communities, Charismatic Masses, parish Masses with Palestrina and Mozart, Tridentine Masses and, of course, the ordinary parish celebration with hymns: that city is modern London. Imagine a city where the Catholics are split up into many different house churches, some celebrating a very Jewish liturgy in Aramaic and following the Torah in their daily lives according to the teaching of St Matthew or the *Didache*; some following the teaching of St Mark's Gospel and celebrating in Greek; others who are followers of whoever wrote St John's Gospel and others of St Peter or of St Paul, and all this before a single New Testament had been compiled and recognized by all; and this is first-century Rome: so we have done it before.

Of course, abuses are also bound to increase as people with more enthusiasm than knowledge try to adapt the ceremonial to their own circumstances. The number of allowable variables we have in the modern Mass is bound to result in some unbalanced liturgies. Some kind of overall supervision is necessary to make sure that what is on offer is in accordance with Catholic Tradition and is of reasonable quality, and also that the sheer variety of groups does not result in fragmentation. It seems to me that, both theologically and practically, the best people to do this are the bishops, as they preside over the liturgy with apostolic authority and are the centre of unity in their dioceses, and they are close enough to local circumstances to be able to make informed judgements. This, of course, would be done under the general supervision of the Pope; but lots of rules coming from Rome do not really help. This brings up the relationship between the Papacy and local churches, a question full of theological, pastoral and ecumenical implications, but one too great to try to tackle here.

Catholic Tradition is a Spirit-driven process by which successive generations are introduced into the Mystery of Christ and come to live and understand the Christian life. This process shows two opposite tendencies which are both caused by its very nature, those of *diversification* and of *unity*. Diversification is caused by people of different cultures, philosophies and temperaments who take up the Christian Faith and interpret it from different viewpoints. Unity happens because they all share in the same Christ and in the same means of contact with him. Thus there are four versions of the one Gospel, each with a different approach to this Mystery and its implications, but all parts of one New Testament canon. Sometimes, diversity ignores unity and becomes destructive. At other times, unity suppresses authentic diversity and becomes oppressive or sectarian; but Christian history can be interpreted in the light of this tension between two opposing but necessary tendencies. Once, when society was much more uniform, legitimate diversity led to different versions of Catholicism in different places and cultures. Now, in our incurably pluralistic society, there can be profoundly different orientations in the same street. This is why, when I advocate Mass with the priest facing the people *and* Mass where everyone faces east, and when I am in favour of Neo-Catechumenate liturgy, monastic liturgy, Mass in English, Latin or Old Slavonic, I am simply recognizing this reality. However, pastors have the difficult task of promoting unity while accepting and even indirectly fostering diversity by encouraging liturgical initiative and participation.

If this policy is to have any chance of success, one truth must always be borne in mind: that the unity with our brothers and sisters which we seek in the liturgy on earth is forged in heaven, and it embraces, whether we like it or not, not only those with whom we celebrate, but also all others who take part in the same Eucharist in whatever rite, use or language, anywhere in the world, in whatever century. Every Eucharist that is celebrated is an act of the whole Church across time and space, and gives the lie to all our petty quarrels, disagreements, misunderstandings, tribalisms and schisms which demonstrate to the world that our treasure is kept in earthen vessels. To pit one Eucharist against another can only be done by people who do not understand the Eucharist. Once we recognize that a Eucharist is real, we recognize all who celebrate it as our brothers and sisters in the faith, indeed as concelebrants in our Eucharist by celebrating their own; and we are united to them, not by the laws of men or by similar customs and tastes or theological points of view, but by the power of the Spirit who is the power of the Eucharist. This is true Catholic unity in true Catholic diversity, and must be an evident factor in a Church which strives to do the will of God on earth as it is done in heaven.

Chapter Twelve

The Liturgy of Life

When I was in the Fifth Form, I read *Elected Silence* by Thomas Merton, and it changed the direction of my life. Up till then, I was going to be either a journalist or a secular priest, then I was going to be just a secular priest; and then I read Thomas Merton and decided I wanted to be a monk, perhaps a Cistercian. What held me back was my attraction to pastoral work. Well, there was Belmont, the English Benedictine monastery in Herefordshire where I was at school. I knew that it also has parishes under its care; but Belmont seemed to me to be a milk-and-water compromise, neither fish nor fowl. Boys of sixteen like extremes; or, at least, they need to dream; they want a goal to aim at, something clear and uncompromising; and Belmont was too prosaic, too ordinary, too concerned with the practical details of life. Then I read *Christ, The Ideal of the Monk* by Columba Marmion. What stuck with me was his chapter on Obedience, and how we follow in Christ's footsteps by being obedient unto death. I also came to know Fr Luke Waring of Belmont who became my confessor. He lent me *Self-Abandonment to Divine Providence* by Jean-Pierre de Caussade, a Jesuit, and my mind was made up. I had found my dream, my goal; it was clear, uncompromising and made sense. I decided to join Belmont. Where else, I thought, could you be a contemplative monk, a parish priest or a school-master, all within the same community at the behest of the abbot? I cannot claim I have always lived up to it, because I would be a saint by now if I had; but it has never ceased to be my goal, and it has made complete sense of the life I am attempting to live. De Caussade's teaching on Self-Abandonment has given me and many other English Benedictines a sense of continuity and coherence, in spite of the ups and downs and the radical changes of lifestyle. Hence I must include one chapter on this simple but demanding way to God, linking his teaching with the theme of this book.

All creatures have a radical relationship with God, because we are sustained in existence by God's love, by the love of the Blessed Trinity, Father, Son, and Holy Spirit. 'All life, all holiness comes from you [the Father] through your Son, Jesus Christ our Lord, by the working of the Holy Spirit' (Eucharistic Prayer III). Withdraw that love from something and it falls into non-existence. This means that every creature and every situation is filled with God's active presence, if only because they are real. De Caussade writes about the treasure which is God's will, God's love:

> Do not ask me what is the secret of finding this treasure? There is no secret. This treasure is everywhere. It is offered to us at every moment in every place. All creatures, both friendly and hostile, pour it out with prodigality and make it pervade every faculty of our body and soul, right to the depths of our heart. We have only to open our mouths and they will be filled. Divine activity floods the whole universe; it pervades all creatures; it flows over them. Wherever they are it is there; it precedes, accompanies and follows them. We have but to allow ourselves to be carried forward on the crest of its waves.[1]

God is Creator, and everything and every moment manifests his creativity in some way or other, simply by existing or happening. If we wish to be creative, then we can either set out to express ourselves, or we can reach another level of creativity by submitting our own creativity to his and allow him to be creative through us. The builders of Chartres, Canterbury and York knew that. They built their cathedrals according to principles they found in creation and were content to be anonymous; but these churches are masterpieces, and it is still a spiritual experience just to walk around them. Visiting medieval churches in the towns and villages of Europe show that this anonymous artistic greatness was very widespread. Not many of us are artists, but all of us can look for the divine will in the ordinary circumstances of our lives and, by responding positively to that will, can, in Mother Teresa's words, do something beautiful for God.

Against this process is self-will: 'Those who find their life will lose it, and those who lose their life for my sake will find it' (Matt. 10:39). To centre our lives on our own needs, feelings or satisfaction, to the exclusion of God, is to miss the most important and beautiful dimension of the world we live in, its relationship with God; but, in order to see creation in this dimension, we need a certain detachment from it. However, once this detachment is achieved within the context of our seeking God, we come to love creation with a greater, profounder and more constant love than ever before.

Hence all people, events, situations, of any type at all, can be manifestations of God's presence and those people, events and situations that are a part of our lives are messages to us by which we know the will of God for us. As it is God's love that sanctifies us, it is not doing our duty in itself that makes us holy, but the Holy Spirit's action in us while, in union with Christ, we respond in faith to do the Father's will. Hence, if it is my job to cook the dinner, but I want to say the rosary with my friends, cooking the dinner will contribute to my holiness, and saying the rosary will not fulfil its purpose. If someone escapes from his obligations at home by helping the parish priest in the parish, the aid he gives to the parish priest in no way contributes to his growth in holiness because he will meet God only in the domestic chores. If he uses his family or his work as an excuse to neglect his duty to God in prayer or to his neighbour, then his work in the house no longer sanctifies him because God invites him to pray or beckons him through his neighbour. Archbishop Romero protesting and opposing the injustices in his country, Mother Teresa helping the poor, the monk in his cell, the mother getting her children ready for school, the husband driving to work in the morning, in so far as they are doing what they are doing because it is the will of God, are all engaged in the liturgy of life.

If God is Creator, he is also Redeemer in Christ 'and in him all things hold together' (Col. 1:17). This means that the cosmic Christ is everywhere, and *all* people, events, situations, of any type at all, can be manifestations of Christ's presence. However, as the appearances of the risen Christ show us in the Gospels, to recognize him is not automatic: it is a *gift*. We have to be addressed like Mary Magdalene at the tomb (John 29:16), or, like the two who were going to Emmaus, have our 'eyes ... opened' at the breaking of bread (Luke 24:31): we need Christ to manifest himself to us in word and sacrament. Once this happens, the way is open to detect his presence and his will in every situation.

The Eucharist remains 'the source and summit of the Christian life',[2] and an ordinary Christian life, authentically lived, is going to reflect the pattern seen in the Mass.

We have already seen that, having been 'obedient unto death', Christ exercises his priesthood by being the human vehicle in creation of the two-way movement of the Holy Spirit; he is the acceptable face of humanity before God, and the human face of God before humankind. He is present with his transforming Spirit in every place and moment. A member of the Church exercises his own priestly role in Christ's name by seeking to do God's will in union with Christ in his sacrifice and this seeking becomes his epiclesis: the Holy Spirit, invoked in the Eucharist on the Church, answers the Church's prayer, not only within the Mass, but also whenever Christians are open to his action, and in this instance, by transforming the situation in which the Christian finds himself into a means of further communion with Christ. It does not matter what kind of situation it is: it can be a positive one like falling in love or a happy family life, or a negative one, like the experience of Maximilian Kolbe and Edith Stein in Auschwitz, or something in between; it can be exciting or boring, extraordinary or humdrum. Whatever type of situation it is, it becomes a means by which God enters into history through the faith response of the Christian, and the Christian is made by the Spirit a means of salvation for others who share the situation with him. Jean Pierre de Caussade wrote:

> Would to God that kings and their ministers, princes of the Church and of the world, priests, soldiers, tradesmen and labourers, in a word, all men, understood how easy it is for them to attain great holiness. They have only to fulfil the simple duties of the Catholic faith and of their state in life, to accept with submission the crosses that go with these duties, and to submit with faith and love to the designs of Providence in everything that is constantly being presented to them to do and to endure, without searching for anything themselves.[3]

While we remain only partly Christian, all this remains a theory that we can so easily forget. However, when, through grace and by dint of much effort, we attain *purity of heart*, we become aware of Christ in everything, and we respond to him in love. This awareness, when our faith pierces the veil of things and rests in Christ with the Father beyond all phenomena, Thomas Merton calls *natural contemplation*. By the action of the Spirit, this is a continuation of that communion we enjoy in the Mass and can lead us into the highest contemplative prayer. As an

English Benedictine monk, I have been a student, a teacher, a chaplain, a pastor, a missionary and a theology teacher in a contemplative monastery. Trying to leave aside self-will and to fix my attention on Christ in the 'sacrament of the present moment' whatever the circumstances, has given me a unity of purpose which has only been interrupted by my sins. It can do the same for anyone who takes up the challenge. Sunday Mass then becomes, not an interruption in a secular week, but the climax of a week in which we have shared in the Christian liturgy of life, in which our lives have become an extension of the Mass we celebrate, in which the whole universe has become for us a sacrament of the risen Christ '*in which Christ is all in all*' (Col. 3:11).

Nevertheless it is helpful, if we wish to see Christ where he is only implicitly present, also to seek him where he explicitly reveals himself. Their Holy Hour before the Blessed Sacrament every day, where the consecrated host has no other reason for its existence than to manifest Christ's presence, helps Mother Teresa's Missionaries of Charity to see Christ in people in the streets and among the bedpans, even when the peoples' behaviour does not remind the sisters of the Jesus whom they represent. The sisters say that they would never be able to see Christ in the poor with such immediacy if they did not see Christ also in the Blessed Sacrament as well. To see Christ in the present moment in our ordinary secular lives, even in our ordinary religious lives, we need to have frequent recourse to him, in himself and for himself. If we are looking for him, Christ can always be found in *lectio divina* or the meditative reading of Scripture, in the Blessed Sacrament, and in icons. Let us now turn our attention to these.

Notes
1. Jean-Pierre de Caussade, *Self-Abandonment to Divine Providence* (Fontana, Collins), p. 36.
2. *Catechism of the Catholic Church* (Geoffrey Chapman, 1994), §1324.
3. See n. 1 above.

Chapter Thirteen

Lectio Divina

One of the fruits of the renewal of the Church in the Holy Spirit for which Pope John XXIII prayed before the Second Vatican Council is the rediscovery of *lectio divina*, the classical way of reading sacred Scripture, not as a text about God or as a record of the beliefs of those who wrote it, but as the Word of God. A presupposition that the Church has traditionally taken for granted is that God actually wants to reveal himself to us, wants to enter into dialogue with us, not only in the liturgy, but constantly. Jesus Christ, as the human face of God which is turned towards us, and as the acceptable face of humanity in the depth of the Blessed Trinity, makes this dialogue possible because it takes place in the Church through the operation of the Holy Spirit. The Dogmatic Constitution on Divine Revelation (*Dei Verbum*) states:

> In the sacred books, the Father who is in heaven meets his children with great love and speaks with them; and the force and power in the word of God is so great that it remains the support and energy of the Church, the strength of faith for her sons, the food of the soul, the pure and perennial source of spiritual life. Consequently, these words are perfectly applicable to sacred Scripture, 'For the word of God is living and efficient' (Heb. 4:12).[1]

The holy Synod earnestly and specifically urges all the Christian faithful, especially religious, to learn by the frequent reading of the divine Scriptures the 'excelling knowledge of Jesus Christ' (Phil. 3:8). 'For ignorance of the Scriptures is ignorance of Christ.' Therefore, they should gladly put themselves in touch with the sacred text itself, whether it be through the liturgy, rich in the divine word, or through devotional reading, or through instructions suitable for the purpose and other aids which, in our time, are commendably available everywhere, thanks to the approval and active support of the shepherds of the Church. And let them remember that prayer should accompany the reading of sacred Scripture, so that God and man may talk together; for 'we speak to him when we pray; we hear him when we read the divine sayings.'[2]

Before the invention of the printing press, people thought that books were a means by which minds meet: they were a form of frozen speech in which the author put down his ideas in the form of symbols which the reader would know and be able to interpret at any time. There was always an author behind a book and a reader interpreting it. It did not exist independently of minds, and reading it became a dialogue between author and reader. Then came the printing press and the illusion that texts have ideas of their own, independently of the context in which they are written and read. For the Fathers of the Church, it was axiomatic that the Scriptures are the Word of God only within a certain context. There is a gap between the Word of God as a divine Person and the word of God as sacred Scripture; a gap that can only be spanned by the Holy Spirit. Hence sacred Scriptures are the Word of God because Christ speaks through them; and this happens only when the Holy Spirit is active in his people, the Church. Without the Spirit the Scripture can be considered as sacred texts, but not as the Word of God. Regarded simply as texts, we see that there are all kinds of different views, not all of them compatible with one another, expressed in the Bible. Some of them, when isolated as views of the individual writer, are downright wrong. It is only with the action of the Holy Spirit that the Scriptures become a unity which reflects the face of Christ, which Christ can use to contact us and which we can use to contact him; and, according to St Irenaeus, only the Church can see this image of Christ and interpret the Scripture correctly, because only the Church has the *charisma veritatis* (the charism of truth). In the words of Nicholas Cabasilas who echoes St Irenaeus, it is only with the Spirit that the sacred Scripture becomes 'an icon of Christ'.

The Old Testament, as its name implies, is sacred Scripture when it reflects the covenant relationship between God and the Jewish People. It, together with the New Testament, also reflects the relationship between God and the Church which has been achieved in Christ. These relationships are not based on the Bible: the opposite is the case. Outside these relationships, the Bible is a mere collection of texts. The relationship between the Jewish People and God, and the relationship that the Christian Church has with God in Christ, have been brought about and are sustained by the Holy Spirit; and the Bible achieves its potential to be the word of God only within the context of these relationships. Within its proper context, which is the liturgy of the Church and in *lectio divina*, God speaks to us in Christ just as truly as he spoke to Moses on Mount Sinai, while we respond in psalms and canticles and hymns as did David before the Ark of the Covenant, but with a closer relationship because we respond in Christ. We have spoken much about the liturgy, so let us now turn to the practice of *lectio divina*.

You may have often seen Evangelicals on television waving big bibles around as they preach – our faith cries out to be expressed as dramatically as possible because the truth of the Gospel is so enormous and the words we use to express it are so weak in comparison – but the truth is that, while the Biblical texts remain within the covers of a Bible of whatever size, they are like seeds in a bag, waiting to be sown. Nothing is so useless than a large Bible, until it is opened and its contents enter our heart. Then it has all the force and none of the destructive power of a hydrogen bomb. Little wonder then that monasteries which adopted the meditative reading of Scripture as their chief occupation came to be considered as centres of spiritual power, not unlike nuclear power stations in secular Britain, but without contamination.

However, as the Reformation protested and as Catholics have discovered, you don't need to be a monk or a nun to practise *lectio divina*. Cardinal Martini could fill his cathedral in Milan with young people, eager for the word of God, as he led them, step by step, through the process of *lectio divina*. The Managhue Benedictine Apostolic Movement in Chile, a lay movement which, rather unexpectedly looks to Ampleforth in England for its inspiration, has made *lectio divina* its central observance; and it teaches it to the children in the schools it runs. Therefore, if you wish to be a spiritual power-house rather than a spiritual wimp, this practice is highly recommended.

The first step is preparatory: it is to know that we are about to enter a dialogue with the Lord. We are people of unclean minds, of unclean lips; and the ground has to be prepared for the seed to be sown. It must be tilled by repentance and by training the mind to be docile and our will to be in *synergy* with that of the Spirit. We must approach the word of God with the mind of Mary who exclaimed, 'Here am I, the servant of the Lord; let it be with me according to your word' (Luke 1:38).

We must be well aware that we are not, at this moment, studying Scripture, nor reading it in a spirit of curiosity. It is better to do our studying of the chosen passage before we start *lectio divina* so that we can concentrate on our meeting with the Lord during the allotted time. We must be mindful that the Lord is speaking to us. Fr

Michael Casey OCSO has written of mindfulness:

> Mindfulness of God ... appears as a hidden factor which changes the quality of what is done. Actions performed in mindfulness somehow have the power to produce a disproportionate effect on the recipient. A cup of cold water given in mindfulness becomes a torrent of salvation which cleanses ... both giver and receiver.

I begin by sitting in solitude in such a way that I am neither distracted by discomfort nor tempted to go to sleep. I become mindful that I am in God's presence; he is all around me, in the very air I breathe. I invoke the Holy Spirit, asking him to bring about a true relationship of love between God and myself. There are four classical ingredients in *lectio divina*; they are not really steps, though they are sometimes treated as such.

The first is *lectio* (reading). You may choose the Sunday readings or a book of the Old Testament one day and of the New Testament the next. You may start by choosing a favourite passage to practise on; but, when you make it a daily event, it is better to let the liturgy choose the passage for you or to read a book from beginning to end. However, on a particular day, it doesn't matter how long the passage is. It may be only a few lines, or it may be a chapter.

The second step is *meditatio* (rumination). If any text strikes you, and you think you can meditate on its meaning for you and respond to it in prayer or turn it into a prayer, or if it simply motivates you to bask in the goodness of God or hits you in any other way, let it. Do not feel you have to continue reading the passage, just to finish it, nor that you have to keep to some kind of programme. Let a text that speaks to you enter deep into your heart, not so much thinking *about* it as tasting it, savouring it, ingesting it, memorizing it, so that you can regurgitate it at odd moments during the day, prolonging the moment of communion. You are not, at this time, analyzing the text. You are not mastering it, taming it, letting it fit into some theological scheme of your own. You are allowing it to master you, allowing it to speak to you without any attempt on your part to dictate to it what it should say to you, allowing the light of Christ to illumine your soul by means of it. Sometimes, it becomes clear to you during this exercise that things in your life must change if you are to progress in union with him in whose presence you are.

The third step is *oratio* (prayer). God has spoken to you. You may now speak to him, turning the text into a prayer, articulating in this form any insight you have received. There is no set time for this: better that it be short and pure than long-winded and full of distractions.

Contemplatio is not a step at all. It is quietly resting in God's presence, *being with God* rather than doing anything. It is normally placed after *oratio* (prayer), but you may well be led to it while taking part in the *meditation*. It may be short; it may be long; it may be interspersed with short prayers or may lead you on to read further. On some days, or in some circumstances, this contemplative bit may be impossible. It is a *gift*. We can make ourselves ready for it, but we cannot make it happen. If it happens, Glory to God! If it doesn't, Glory to God again!! God knows what he is doing.

The important thing is that *lectio divina* must be practised every day, for a set time, and, if possible, at the same time each day. You may think that everything is superb on the first day; but the truth is that you have much to learn on listening to God. Much of the time we listen, but only really hear ourselves. This 'method', if method it is, cannot be separated from our war against our own egoism. Remember that these four ingredients are not really steps, at least, not as you progress. They tend to interpenetrate each other; and it may be difficult to tell when one ends and the other begins. However, there is a certain rhythm: reading Scripture is *active*, something we do, while ruminating on the passage is more *receptive*, waiting on God to enlighten us through the text. Praying is again *active*, something we do towards God; and *Contemplation* is more receptive, in that we become more and more mindful of God's loving presence and, more and more, we simply drink it in.

This classic form of *lectio divina* must be distinguished from another, very similar activity which often goes under the same name. In fact, the other practice is a version of the See, Judge, Act which was introduced into the Church by the Young Christian Workers. In this case the 'See' is the reading of the sacred text; the 'Judge' is applying the chosen text to a situation which needs changing; and then this leads on to the 'Act' which is formulated in a prayer. This is often done in a group, and the success or failure of the exercise depends on whether the 'Act' is performed successfully or not.

This is an excellent means of finding out what God wants us to do; but it differs from classical *lectio divina* both in its purpose and in the means. *Lectio divina* is undertaken to increase our union with God and, if and when God wills, to lead us to contemplation. It is individualistic in that its context is the individual's personal relationship with God, and it has no other purpose outside that. It is true that it may lead to some activity with others; but this is not the criterion by which it is judged. Remember that, in the classic view, community and individuality in prayer are not opposed to one another. In fact, our experience of Christ in community is as strong and profound as our one-to-one relationship with him permits it to be. On the other hand, we have a one-to-one relationship with Christ because we have been baptized and because we receive him in Holy Communion and have become 'flesh of his flesh and bones of his bones', and the sacraments are communal actions. In contrast, the other kind of *lectio divina* is geared to action. In the classical type we ruminate on the text without trying to get it to do things, caressing God who speaks through it:

in the other kind, we use it to guide us into some kind of activity to change things for the better. These two ways are not absolutely exclusive and can be practised at different times by the same person according to circumstances, but they are not the same thing; and the *lectio* that is geared to action cannot be a substitute for the contemplative kind among people who have chosen *lectio divina* as a way to God.

Reading the Scriptures as Word of God leads us to have a different attitude towards them. Scholars may wish to find tthe original meaning of a text, and this is a good thing and can teach us much; but, as Word of God, it can have many meanings, according to the needs of the reader and the context in which he reads it. Let us take as an example the text, 'You are Peter, and on this rock I will build my Church.' Its original meaning is important, and scholars are right to do everything possible to uncover it. But it is more than a text: it is the word of God and God speaks to those who read it with faith; and, as such, it has had several meanings, both new and old (Matt. 13:52). We all know how it has motivated the popes to seek the unity and spiritual health of the Church. In the Syrian Rite it is the gospel reading for the ordination of a bishop. St John Chrysostom, who lived in an age when the Church was preoccupied with questions concerning the Incarnation, sees this passage as confirming the truth that the Incarnation is the very basis of Christianity. In none of these interpretations are we dealing with the text abstracted from the context in which it was read. All three interpretations were accepted by those who held them as the Lord illuminating the situation in which they lived their Christian lives by means of the text. It is a waste of time and a misunderstanding of the Word of God to set these interpretations against one another.

The real question, considering that in the Church the whole is present in each part by the power of the Holy Spirit, is why what is so obvious to the Catholic Church in the West is not also seen with the same joy in the East. My own guess is that, for a long time before the schism, the East and the West simply did not love one another; that this led to lack of empathy, and thus to a loss of mutual understanding. It is not for nothing that the recitation of the Creed is associated with the Sign of Peace in the Byzantine Mass. Faith is knowledge that springs from love; the love that God bears us, and the love that we have for God and our neighbour which is in *synergy* with the love of God. Love ventures forth first, and understanding follows. A truly Catholic interpretation would be the sum total and synthesis of all the meanings that are the product of participating in the sacred liturgy and its extension in *lectio divina*. Scholars could come up with another interpretation that they could say is the original. Let them, and then we shall add it to the rest; but it will not nullify the meanings associated with the text by the Church at prayer. One of the classical differences between Protestantism and Catholicism is that Protestants regard the text of the Bible as standing on its own, over and sometimes against the Church, while Catholics regard it as the Word of God in so far as it expresses the communication between God and the Church brought about by the Spirit. This communication pre-exists the New Testament and forms the context in which it was written and in which it must be understood.

I have chosen 'You are Peter', but could have chosen many other texts, such as 'Give us this day our daily [*epiousion*] bread'. '*Epiousion*' may be '*ep-iousion*' or '*epi-ousion*' If it is the first, the root verb is the Greek verb for 'to come' or 'to go'; if it is the second, it comes from the verb 'to be'. If it is the first, its most probable meaning is 'bread of the Coming', ('bread of the kingdom', perhaps), or 'tomorrow's bread'. If it comes from the verb 'to be', then it can mean, somewhat improbably as an original meaning, 'super-substantial bread' (the Eucharist?); 'sufficient bread'; and, just possibly, 'daily bread'. It is clear that the New Testament authors are using Greek as though it were Hebrew; and it is likely that all these meanings are meant. Having an Old Testament in Hebrew, which has a limited vocabulary and where words have multiple meanings, the Jews revelled in ambiguity and used it to say several things in one sentence. This was true, even when they wrote in Greek; and St John's Gospel, for instance, makes ample use of ambiguity to mean several things at once. Hence, the idea that Bible texts can have several meanings is not foreign to the Bible itself. It only becomes a problem when the text replaces the Church's rule of faith and is expected to be a source of unity in belief, a role which it is not equipped to fulfil.

Scholars may also argue on which text is the most authentic when there are various versions from which to choose. Again, this is a very valuable exercise and should help us to understand our faith; but the question of the most authentic text does not arise when we are practising *lectio divina*. It is enough that the text has been used in the context where God speaks to the Church and the Church speaks to God 'in Christ', in the liturgy and in *lectio divina*, and has thus been recognized as the word of God by the Church. Hence the Fathers adopted all variations as allowable and useful in the dialogue between God and humanity.

The practice of *lectio divina* should become a regular part of our Christian lives, a means to extend the relationship we have with God in the liturgy into our everyday lives. This way of prayer is not difficult in itself, and can lead us into the highest forms of contemplation: all we need is perseverance and the grace of God.

Notes
1. *Dei Verbum* 21, *The Documents of Vatican II* (Geoffrey Chapman, London and Dublin, 1966), p. 125.
2. *Dei Verbum* 25, ibid. p. 127.

Chapter Fourteen

The Bread of the Presence

In the Temple in Jerusalem there were kept within the sanctuary twelve loaves of bread, called 'bread of the Presence' or 'bread of the Face'. They were placed before the Holy of Holies at the beginning of the week, and consumed by the priests at the week's end. After being baked, they were placed on stone tables to await their use in the sanctuary, but, once inside, they were put on a table of gold because they became holy only after being placed before the Lord. Their function seems to have been a mute plea to God on behalf of Israel, and their holiness came from the Presence and its blessing which they absorbed. It was this bread which David and his followers ate because they were hungry, but this obliged them to live holy lives and to keep themselves ritually clean for a whole year afterwards. There is a certain parallel between this practice of keeping the 'bread of the Presence' and that of the Catholic Church in keeping the Blessed Sacrament in a tabernacle. Remember that the theological equivalent of the Temple in Christianity is the Eucharistic assembly, and that the bread has been made holy by the Father in Christ by the power of the Spirit. It is truly the 'bread of the Face' because Christ is the human face of God, and it is a mute plea to the Father for the good of the Church because Christ is the acceptable face of humanity in the presence of the Father. It is the reality of which the Jewish practice was a mere shadow.

There are liturgists who will immediately protest that devotion to Christ as *presence* took over in the Middle Ages from the true and classical role of Christ in the Eucharist as *gift* to the Father and to us in the form of bread and wine. They point out that in the Middle Ages, the main purpose of the consecration was to make Christ present, and the main means for lay people to profit from his presence was through adoration. After Vatican II, the main emphasis has become our communal sharing in Christ's body and blood, thus forming us into his body. Theologians since the Council have put the doctrine of the Real Presence within the context of communion sacrifice rather than as something that stands by itself, independently of the Eucharistic action. No wonder then that such practices as Benediction of the Blessed Sacrament, and Forty Hours have been dying out. In some parts of the States, they speak of *old church* and *new church*, and devotion to the presence of Christ in the Blessed Sacrament is definitely *old church* and to be discouraged on every possible occasion. The Mass is essentially a *communal* meal, while devotion to the Blessed Sacrament is essentially *individualistic*.

Yet devotion to the Blessed Sacrament is coming back; it is an important part of some of the most successful renewal groups and of the new religious communities, and it has been strongly advocated by two popes after the Council and especially during the Year of the Eucharist. Several of the parishes in Lima are building chapels to expose the Blessed Sacrament regularly, so that people can come off the streets into a calm and silent atmosphere to pray when the main church is empty; and I know of one village church in the countryside where the people have built a Blessed Sacrament chapel. Several parishes in Lima practise perpetual adoration of the Blessed Sacrament, with ordinary lay people watching before the exposed Sacrament every day and every night throughout the year. This is not a relic of some past age – there is nothing *old church* about it – it is a new practice, introduced into parishes where the Vatican II liturgy is very much alive. Is all this a departure from a truly liturgical spirit?

It is true that the traditional devotion to the Blessed Sacrament was very individualistic. However, *communal* and *individualistic* devotion are not exclusive opposites: they are complementary and need each other to survive. I spent one and a half years in a 'liberation theology' parish up in the Andes and noticed that, although individual devotion was not encouraged and evangelization was geared to the transformation of society, the only people who threw themselves into the community projects, whether they served their self-interest or not, were those with a strong, quite old-fashioned devotion to Christ and Our Lady. Those who took part without this devotion simply did not have the spiritual stamina to keep going. The Cistercian tradition tells us that the spiritual life has two poles, community and solitude. Without each person having a one-to-one relationship with Christ, community becomes a crowd or only superficially Christian; and without a strong sense of community, individualistic devotion can become a selfish indulgence. Together, community and solitude strengthen each other because we meet Christ both in the community and in the depths of our own hearts; and one dimension cannot be really genuine without the other. If this is so, then an individualistic devotion to Christ in the Blessed Sacrament outside the Mass should strengthen and deepen rather than weaken our Christian community and participation in the liturgy.

The division between *old Church* and *new Church* is un-Catholic. The Church depends on the Holy Spirit for its very existence; and the evidence of the Spirit's presence is found in holiness down the ages. Each generation has its limitations and blind spots, and each generation produces its saints who are evidence of the Spirit at work; we cannot afford to forget their testimony if we wish to strive for sanctity ourselves. One practice that has been an integral part of the relation between Christ and his saints in the last few hundred years is devotion to Christ in the Blessed Sacrament. Edith Stein (St Teresa Benedicta of the Cross) put great emphasis on the Church as Body of Christ and on the communal aspect of Catholic life, but she received much spiritual sustenance from devotion to Jesus in the Blessed Sacrament, and it was a constant factor in her spirituality. Her last act in her convent as she was being arrested by the Nazis was a quick visit to the tabernacle; and she is only one example among many.

To mention three others, all in one breath, who in the twentieth century were known for their holiness and for whom devotion to the Blessed Sacrament was an important component in that holiness, here is a quotation from Dorothy Day talking about Pierre Maurin, who founded with her the *Catholic Worker Movement*, and his admiration for Charles de Foucauld:

> I first heard of Charles de Foucauld from Pierre Maurin in the early thirties, when the work of the *Catholic Worker* was just beginning. The biography by René Bazin appeared in 1920 and Peter had read it and spoke often of men and women living in the world a consecrated life of manual labour, poverty and adoration. Actually he was speaking of secular institutes, though they were not known as such at the time. He himself spent an hour a day in adoration, and I have told in my book *The Long Loneliness* how when I first met him and he proposed the *Catholic Worker Movement*, I went to meet him in a parish church and found him absorbed before the Holy Eucharist, so absorbed that I too sat in the church waiting for him for almost an hour.[1]

Carlo Carretto, in his book *Letters from the Desert*, writes of praying alone before the Blessed Sacrament in a cave in the Sahara:

> A hamper of bread, a few dates, some water, the Bible. A day's march: a cave. A priest celebrates Mass; then goes away, leaving in the cave, on an altar of stones, the Eucharist. Thus for a week one remains alone with the Eucharist exposed day and night. Silence in the desert, silence in the cave, silence in the Eucharist. One's whole natural strength rebels against it.
>
> One would prefer to carry stones in the sun. The senses, memory, imagination, all are repressed. Faith alone triumphs, and faith is hard, dark, stark.
>
> To place oneself before what seems to be bread and to say, 'Christ is there living and true,' is pure faith.
>
> But there is nothing more nourishing than pure faith, and prayer in faith is real prayer.
>
> 'There is no pleasure in adoring the Eucharist,' one novice used to say to me. But it is precisely this renunciation of all desire to satisfy the senses that makes prayer strong and real. One meets God beyond the senses, beyond the imagination, beyond nature.[2]

Not only do people on the way to great sanctity find sustenance in devotion to the Blessed Sacrament, but also, in my experience, a surprising number of people have become Catholics because they have entered a church and have been gobsmacked by the sense of presence which they associated with the tabernacle. When Catholics return to the sources, it is to the activity of the Holy Spirit down the ages, from Jesus and his disciples to the present day, that they return, because the Spirit is the real Source of all life in the Church and belongs equally to all ages. To dismiss practices as *old church*, especially when they have been a means by which the Spirit has led people to holiness, is to ignore the true nature of the Church, which is Christ's body because of the Spirit's constant activity. It is superficial to subject Christian practices to the laws of fashion. The only criterion worth having is that of holiness: does this practice help people to love God and neighbour or not?

The very concrete belief of the Fathers provides ample justification for our devotion to the Blessed Sacrament. For example, St John Chrysostom wrote:

> The Magi adored the body lying in the manger ... it is not now lying in a crib that I see thee but upon the altar ... This is the same body that was covered in blood, pierced by the spear, pouring forth the saving streams of blood and water, for the whole world. Christ soared up from the depths of the abyss in dazzling light and leaving his rays there he went up to his throne in heaven. It is that body he gives us to hold and to eat now.[3]

'See', 'hold', 'eat', and 'body' are very concrete terms, but no more concrete than those of St John, 'We declare to you ... what we have seen with our eyes, what we have looked at and touched with our hands, concerning the word of life' (1 John 1:1). Some theologians lose themselves in abstractions. Christian revelation has elements of *seeing*, of *touching* and *holding* and *eating* as well as *hearing*. Too often the liturgy is words, words, words, among Christians who are starved of seeing, touching and holding. We shall see in the next chapter that Eastern Christians have developed the use of the *icon* to extend Christ's visible presence in the Church beyond the celebration of the liturgy. However, in spite of the seventh ecumenical council's official acceptance by the pope, its teaching on icons was rejected by the Frankish bishops and was never fully accepted by Western theologians, even though popular religion among the poor was very similar to that of the Greeks because they had their shrines and holy wells and statues and holy pictures. However, in the towns where, presumably, the influence of theologians was stronger, the people still wanted to *see* as well as to hear and believe, and the Blessed Sacrament came to be used as a window into eternity, doing for Western Christians what the icon does for the Greeks.

Although seeing was also a substitute for communion, we who go to communion with regularity can only benefit from this other secondary use of the Blessed Sacrament discovered by our medieval ancestors. 'He looks at me, and I look at him,' said the old peasant to St Jean Mary Vianney. It would not harm us to do the same.

At the same time, we can benefit from the example and spirituality of the East where the tabernacle containing the Eucharistic Presence which is the object of their adoration is the tabernacle of the heart. When we receive Christ in Holy Communion, he remains within us by the power of the Spirit, unless thrust out by sin. Once we cut through our pride and self-sufficiency, we can reach him in our inward being and commune with him at any time and in every place. These two types of Eucharistic devotion are not opposed to each other, and mutually support one another if allowed to do so.

Notes

1. Dorothy Day, 'Retreat' in *Catholic Worker* (August 1959), 3, 7 and 8.
2. Carlo Carretto, *Letters from the Desert* (Darton, Longman & Todd, 1972), p. 12.
3. John Chrysostom, *Homily on First Corinthians*, 24, 5 (PG 61, 204), *Homily on Matthew*, 50, 3 (PG 58, 507), *Homily on I Corinthians*, 24, 4 (PG 61, 203–4), quoted from Olivier Clément, *The Roots of Christian Mysticism* (New, City, 1993), p. 109.

Chapter Fifteen

Images

One of the things that takes a great deal of getting used to in Latin American *religiosidad popular* is the important role that images have in the minds, hearts and practices of the Catholic faithful. There are shrines in practically every diocese, each one centred on a statue or picture; and people go on pilgrimage to that shrine, men, women and children, walking for days, sometimes carrying heavy crosses; and some pilgrims do the final distance on their knees. Touching and kissing the image are important to the pilgrims, and it is common to buy a bunch of candles, to light them and to stand in prayer before the image until the candles burn down to one's fingers. In the week before the feast of *Senor Cautivo* (the Captive Christ) in Ayabaca, 2,700 metres up in the Andes, pilgrims can be seen walking along the road, each bearing his or her blanket and water bottle, some carrying babies on their shoulders; most wear a purple headband or armband or something, and a few wear the full purple habit and yellow cord which is special to this devotion. It is an impressive sight. In Lima there is the picture of the 'Lord of the Miracles' which is carried in procession at the end of October. The streets are packed with hundreds of thousands of people, as at the coronation of the Queen in England, and many have walked there from great distances. In the villages also, there are annual *fiestas* centred on the images in their church, and the peasants touch them and kiss them and pray before them. 'If you want to understand popular religion in Peru, read Chaucer,' an American missionary told me when I first arrived. 'It is medieval religion, both for good and bad. The councils of Trent and Vatican I had little impact, and the Spanish who came to South America were medieval Crusaders when the rest of Europe had moved on. For instance, the people go on pilgrimage, just like Chaucer's characters in his Canterbury Tales.'

I used to wonder why these images were so important. Were the people really superstitious? Was there something happening that did not quite fit in to my perspective? It was very difficult to find these things out, because the peasants are often not very good at articulating their faith. They live it, but few can explain it. Then, one day, I met a highly articulate peasant with the imagination to realize what I wanted to know. I asked him about the importance of images. After thinking for a little while, he said, 'When an image receives the blessing of the Church, it becomes for us a manifestation of God's presence, a point of contact between God and us.'

It could have been the Fathers of the second Council of Nicaea speaking. The fathers of that council argued that the Incarnation of Christ had brought about a completely new relationship between the material creation and God, so new that it rendered the old prohibition against images obsolete. In Christ, God and man became one in such a way that 'He who sees me sees the Father'. Since his Ascension into heaven, Christ lives in the Presence of his Father, and in him ' all things hold together' (Col. 1:17). Since that time everything *can* be – and, at the end of things, when there is a new heaven and a new earth, everything *will* be – a symbol of Christ's presence. Whenever we see Christ in anything or anybody, this is part of the process by which God claims back for himself a fallen world; and the painting and use of icons (images) is part of the same process. By them, as well as by the Blessed Sacrament, we prolong into the liturgy of ordinary living the theophany that is the liturgy. However, it is highly probable that the priests who have attended the spiritual needs of these peasants over the years have never learned this in their seminary or read it in their theology books. After the second Council of Nicaea had met to define the Catholic attitude to images in AD 787, although it had the full backing of the pope, its conclusions were rejected by the Frankish bishops under Charlemagne, partly because they had received a faulty text and believed that the council had countenanced idolatry, and partly because it was believed that nothing good could come out of the East. The Pope had to use all his diplomacy to win their reluctant acceptance, but this did not stop another synod from condemning the council at Frankfurt in 790, and another repeating the condemnation in Paris in 828. For the bishops, images were only good as decorations and as means to teach the illiterate. In time, the categories of honour as taught in the council were adopted, but their full significance never became a part of the Western theological tradition. The council's full teaching on the place of images in Christian worship remained in the East, and in western popular religion. Thus, popular religion and liturgy are well integrated in Orthodoxy, while in the West they tended to speak different languages and have grown apart. This separation has affected negatively both the liturgy and the devotions. The process in the West reached its climax after the second Vatican Council when, for many, to be liturgical involved rejecting popular Catholic devotions. I am sure that this was one factor in making Christianity too abstract for the young and in losing the allegiance of the poor and the unlettered because we had stolen their religious language. Thanks be to God, this could not happen in Latin America where the poor are too numerous and reforming clerics too thin on the ground.

To understand the doctrine of the second Council of Nicaea it is necessary to go back to basics, to imagine the risen, ascended Christ at the very centre of all things, exercising his priestly ministry by being the vehicle of the two-way action of the Holy Spirit. By this action, Jesus is the human face of God to us and the acceptable face of humanity to God. This relationship between God and the Church, the new covenant, which is brought about by Christ's ministry, exists at many levels and takes many forms, but it is always a two-way thing, never just in one direction. Through Baptism, we become sharers in this relationship, sharers in the very life of God, together with the angels and saints, and we celebrate it together in the Eucharist. Again, because everything in existence exists by God's Word, anything can become an instrument of this two-way activity of God in which we are involved, though some actions and things are more fitting than others to be symbols of Christ's presence and activity. When something is blessed by the Church, it is moved into the context of this two-way relationship and becomes a vehicle for it. Therefore, icons and other images which have been blessed become ways by which we meet Our Lord, Our Lady and the saints, and they meet us: hence images are much more than simply reminders.

In spite of the fact that God lives 'in unapproachable light and cannot be seen, whom no one has ever seen or can see' (1 Tim. 6:16), there is a visual element in Christian revelation, an anticipation of heaven where 'we will be like him, for we will see him as he is' (1 John 3:2). 'We declare to you ... what we have heard, what we have seen with our eyes, what we have looked at and touched with our hands, concerning the word of life' (1 John 1:1). 'Whoever sees me sees him who sent me' (John 12:45). 'Whoever has seen me has seen the Father' (John 14:9). 'In a little while the world will no longer see me; *but you will see me*; because I live, you also will live' (John 14:19). 'Blessed are the pure in heart, for they will see God' (Matt. 5:8). ' Blessed are your eyes, for they see, and your ears, for they hear. Truly I tell you, many prophets and righteous people longed to see what you see, but did not see it, and to hear what you hear, but did not hear it'

(Matt. 13:17f). 'Master, now you are dismissing your servant in peace, according to your word; for my eyes have *seen* your salvation' (Luke 2:29ff). There is an instinct in Catholicism to use all our senses when we seek God, because God now has a human face which is reflected on the faces of Our Lady and the saints.

If God communicates with us through what is visible by the power of the Spirit, as well as by what is audible, certain questions are raised. For instance, what do the faithful *see* when they go to Mass? What *should* they see which will lead them to be mindful of the truth they are celebrating? What do people from outside the Church *see* when they look at us to remind them of the body of Christ? What should they *see*? The Church is not just an institution such as Freemasonry which celebrates certain rites. We are back to the subject of our first article. What vision do we portray?

Those who *write* icons – (those in the know do not *paint* icons: they *write* them) – know that they are collaborating with the person they are portraying. On the one hand, the person or persons portrayed want to manifest their presence to the Church; and the artist contributes to this project with his painting skills. Painting is accompanied by prayer and fasting, and the artist is very careful not to let his ego step in between the subject and the person who will use the icon. Like the Gospels, icons do not bear the name of the artist. 'The Hospitality of Abraham' was written by the great iconographer A. Rublev, a monk, after twenty years of retreat in silence, during which he did not paint anything. Icon-writing is a vocation, a means of seeking and serving God. Every technique, every detail, every brush-stroke is filled with theological meaning. We are lucky enough to have two iconographers in my community, one at Belmont in England, and one in Peru. Brother Alex in Peru was horrified when a monk who knows nothing of icons wanted him to produce them at a faster rate so that they could earn the monastery much-needed cash. 'Do I have to?' he asked me afterwards. For him the prayer and the slow pace are part and parcel of icon-writing: it is primarily a meeting with God.

Once ready, the icon is blessed with holy water and anointed with chrism, making it a thing of the Church, an instrument of dialogue between heaven and earth. An icon does not make Jesus, Our Lady and the saints present: only the Holy Spirit can do that; but the blessing means that the icon *manifests* the presence of Jesus, Our Lady and the saints. The icon looks distorted because its perspective does not lead to some point behind the picture, but to the heart of the person observing. The eyes of the person normally look at the observer too. The blessing means that, when people stand before the icon in faith, the Spirit brings about a true dialogue between them and the subject of the icon. Because of this, people refer to icons as if they were the persons themselves.

In one week I saw a DVD on the icon of Our Lady of Tikhvin in which a Russian Orthodox priest thanked God for the visit of the Blessed Virgin 'in her icon'; and I heard the prayer of one of our Peruvian monks who had walked for three days on pilgrimage to Ayabaca who thanked Christ at Vespers for having seen him 'in *el Senor Cautivo*'. Central to the shrine of Ayabaca is a statue of Jesus with his hands tied. Such immediacy of language, and the intimate way both Russians and Peruvians touch and kiss their images are justified by an ecumenical council and show us a rich resource for the contact with God once we come to understand it.

On the cover of this book you will see an icon. Mary, dressed in bridal attire, is embracing Jesus who is dead but standing (Rev. 5:6). There is nothing beautiful about either Jesus or Mary, nothing sentimental. Nobody is trying to play on your feelings. Yet the icon is about love, both human and divine. In Old Slavonic there is written, 'Do not cry for me, Mother', and this is the official title of the icon; but its normal name is 'The Bridegroom' or 'The Marriage of the Lamb'. In the background, portrayed without detail in gold, is the Heavenly Jerusalem, come down from heaven as a bride (Rev. 21:1-4). It is gold, to signify the divine light. The city does not need the sun or the moon to shine on it because the glory of God is its light and the Lamb is its lamp (Rev. 21:23). The theme of light continues in the painting of the body of Christ. It is delicately lit up, while his head is not. This reminds us that the Church is Christ's body, and he is its head, and that he did not die for himself but for us: his humiliation (the relative obscurity of the head) is our salvation (the faint shimmering light on the body). Although Mary is the 'mother of all the living' because she is the mother of him who embraces the whole human race in his humanity, her love was only sufficiently deep enough and wide enough to embrace all humanity when she accompanied her son Jesus to his death on the cross. As St Rose of Lima wrote, we grow in the life of the Spirit mainly through tribulation: and it was the same for her. Our destiny too is to become big enough to have a universal love for all creation which reflects the divine love, and that will involve inevitable pain. As Mary clutched her dead son in desolation and faith on the first Good Friday, she also embraced all of us as her children. After this, if Jesus represents us before his Father, Mary represents the Church in our intimate relationship with Jesus. We benefit, not just from our own relationship with Jesus, small and inadequate as it is, because her relationship becomes ours as she clutches his dead body to herself. This is an icon of Jesus and Mary, the second Adam and the second Eve, as they give birth in love to the Church.

The icon was painted by Brother Alex of our monastery in Pachacamac in Peru, and it hangs in our chapel. We sing the *Salve Regina* in front of it before going to bed at night. We also touch it with our hands and look at it with our eyes and honour it with an inclination of the head after every office, because it not only depicts a great mystery, it also manifests that mystery and allows us to participate in it.

When the Holy Spirit takes up residence within us, he transforms our senses so that they become capable of looking through the windows that open into an eternity where they cannot go themselves. The Gospels are full of visual images even when they are painted in words. In imagining them, we are introduced to great mysteries that are above words and too great for our imagination. What is a parable if it is not a visual image expressing a great truth? The visual image of blood and water flowing from the side of the crucified Christ conjures up truths about Christ, about the temple and about the sacraments. The vision is always immeasurably greater than the image, and this is true with icons. They keep presenting us with new aspects of the mystery they depict. Brother Alex wrote the icon with prayer. There was no room for his egoism or even his personality. He was not trying to express himself when he painted it. He knew through faith that Jesus and Mary wish to manifest themselves to us, and it was his task to make this possible through painting the icon.

Our monastery overlooks the fields of the Pachacamac valley, a valley with its own mini-climate, like many places round Lima. About twenty minutes' walk away there is a small village with a convent of six sisters. They belong to a new congregation called 'The Servants of Jesus and Mary'. It is one of several new communities founded in France in recent years which are monastic in inspiration. Their members wear a monastic habit and they do many of the things that people foretold would disappear after Vatican II. Each nun spends an hour before the Blessed Sacrament each day. Although they have a set policy of not encouraging people to join them – 'If God wants us to thrive, he will send recruits' – these sisters, like the other new congregations, have no problem with vocations. They adopted the brown habit of Cistercian lay sisters that was discarded in Trappist convents after it was decided to abolish the lay sisterhood as an entity separate from the nuns in choir, and the first members of this new community did their noviciate in a Trappist monastery. They have received from the Cistercians their love for the Divine Office, their practice of *lectio divina* (the meditative reading of Scripture and the Fathers), and their striving to meet God in contemplation. However, they live among the very poor, and they are dedicated to a particular apostolate. They invite young people to live with them for a minimum of fourteen months and a maximum of two years, and to share in their life of adoration and their compassion for the poor. They make no effort to attract these young people to their own community. All they hope is that the experience will have an impact on their future. Recently in France, four girls who lived with them in this way later joined the 'Community of Bethlehem', another modern French congregation which follows the Carthusian rule and does not lack vocations either. The Servants of Jesus and Mary also have a particular icon, very much like the one that Alex painted, which, they say, depicts the spirit and ideals of their community. In a coincidence which is commonplace for people who try to live by faith, they came to our opening Mass and found the same icon in a place of honour in our chapel. For them it depicts both Mary's intimacy with Jesus and her compassion for suffering, both of which they strive to emulate. They call our icon, 'Our Lady of Compassion'. Icons, like the Scriptural texts, have many meanings, and we can continue to receive through them new meanings and old.

When attempts were made to make a statue of Our Lady of Lourdes, based on the description of her appearance to St Bernadette, the young saint scornfully set them aside as in no way fitting her memory of the Virgin. The statues depicted her in clothes exactly as St Bernadette had described, standing as she described, but no sculptor could make a statue to the saint's satisfaction. Then St Bernadette saw an icon of Our Lady of Perpetual Succour: 'She was like that,' she said. The icon in no way fits St Bernadette's description; but it had something that an attempt to sculpt a statue based on a merely natural description has not. In fact, an icon of the Blessed Virgin has much in common with an apparition in that it is a way that the Blessed Virgin manifests her presence to the Church. For this reason it is painted in prayer; and the faithful who approach it know that they are drawing near to Our Lady Herself.

One advantage that icons have over Western religious pictures is that they belong to an art-form that has developed in the Church and manifests the Church's nature, and they are essentially an instrument of the Church, only making sense because the Church itself is an icon, both an image of and a manifestation of Christ and of creation redeemed by Christ. For this reason, an icon is only a proper icon when it is blessed by the Church. An icon brings together word and image. It is not an icon if it is not a pictorial image; nor is it an icon without words. These words name the icon, telling us something about its basic message. The Church is a living icon. Its community life and its liturgy are meant to be a pictorial image of the Christian Mystery and a means of participating in it, the local community at Mass being the visible part of the whole Church throughout the world and down the ages. According to Jesus, it is the actual visible unity of the Church, united in love by the Holy Spirit, that will show the world that Christ was sent by the Father (John 17:20–4).

Icons exist, not just because they are a means of teaching people who cannot read: nor are they simple reminders to us of past events or of people long dead; they exist because the New Testament itself presents us with images painted in words, images that appeal to our imagination, and are proclamations of the Gospel, even as images in the mind. Chief among them is the image of Christ crucified. As the serpent in the desert was lifted up and cured those who looked on it, so Jesus too was lifted up; and we see him in our mind's eye and accept him and are saved. Different from the religion of Deuteronomy,

God is seen as well as heard. In our day, as in every generation, the proclamation of the Gospel has its visual dimension; and that visual dimension is us, because we are the body of Christ, Christ made visible.

Epilogue

I am bringing you good news of great joy for all the people ...
And they worshipped him, and returned to Jerusalem with great joy
Luke 2, 10; 24:52

We declare to you ... what we have heard, what we have seen with our eyes, what we looked at and touched with our hands, concerning the word of life.
1 John 1:1

Enter into the joy of the Lord.
Matt. 25:21

We were made for God, and our hearts are restless until they find rest in him. Our desire for God is implicit in all our other desires, our need for him implicit in all our other needs. We were made to love and be loved, and God is implicit in all our loves, even when we love out of turn or when our love is distorted in some way. The Good News is that the Life which is implicit in our desire to live can be ours. God loves us and is offering his life to us, the life of the Blessed Trinity, to be our life. God has a human face and meets us at our own level so that he can raise us up to his by grace.

> If God is for us, who is against us? He who did not withhold his own Son, but gave him up for all of us, will he not with him also give us everything else? Who will bring any charge against God's elect? It is God who justifies. Who is to condemn? It is Christ Jesus, who died, yes, who was raised, who is at the right hand of God, who indeed intercedes for us. Who will separate us from the love of Christ? (Rom. 8:31–5).

This being the case, we should be full of joy. St Luke is well aware of the joyous nature of the Good News, and also that many accept it without joy. The two disciples on the way to Emmaus (Luke 24:13–25) knew the whole story but they were sad and quarrelsome when they met Jesus on the road. News of the resurrection did not make them happy, because they had a different agenda from God's. They expected Jesus to overthrow the Romans and establish a free and prosperous Israel. Jesus needed to speak to them sharply and then to give them the necessary insight into God's plan of salvation. Only with a rearrangement of their values which comes from conversion could they then recognize him in the breaking of bread and share in his paschal joy. It is same with us. If we simply share the consumer values of the society we live in and the ambitions of secular people, even though we follow the rules of the Church, the Mass will be a duty, not a joy. The Lord invites us to enter the joy of the Lord, but we shall enter with glum faces. To be really happy, we must change our values and rearrange our priorities: we must be converted. Jesus said, 'The time is fulfilled, and the kingdom of God has come near; repent and believe in the good news.' This repentance is more than sorrow for past sins committed: it is a total change of direction. When this has been done, we become capable of a joy for which all other joys are a preparation or a pale imitation, because what is being accomplished is the reason why we and everything in the universe have been created: we are being united to Christ; we are entering the kingdom.

The Eucharist is the Church's entry into the kingdom.[1] Alexander Schmemann defines *liturgy* as an action by which a group of people become corporately what they could not be as a collection of individuals. It also means a 'ministry' or public office in which a group does something on behalf of the whole community. Thus the *liturgy* of ancient Israel was to prepare the world for the coming of the Messiah. The *liturgy* of the Church is to be the body of Christ and to witness before the world to Christ and the kingdom. In the Mass the Church is taken into the presence of the Father and is transformed by the Spirit into the body of his Son. We listen to Christ's word, pray in and with him, addressing *Abba, Father*, in praise, thanksgiving, repentance and intercession, and we receive him into ourselves, becoming flesh of his flesh, bones of his bones. We are then sent into the world to bear witness to 'what we have heard, what we have seen with our eyes, what we have looked at and touched with our hands'. Primarily as Church, but also individually as members of the Church, we become an *icon* of Christ. We become visible to the world as icon of Christ by the quality of our love, and we become invisible to the world and cease to be effective as an icon of Christ by our lack of love.

Just as an icon is mainly a visual image but needs words to explain or indicate the meaning of the icon, so, in the words of St Francis of Assisi, we must bear witness to the Gospel by the quality of our lives and, when necessary, by our words.

Back in the Valley of Pachacamac, we have the task of being an icon of Christ as a religious community by being true to our vocation as a Benedictine monastery. This means that that we try to love God and our neighbour according to the Rule of St Benedict, leaving to the Holy Spirit how we will bear witness to Christ in the world at large. Across the valley, the Servants of Jesus and Mary are doing something similar; and a few miles away the Cistercian nuns in Lurin are doing the same. Wearing our habits helps in our task to act as icons of Christ because this points beyond ourselves without our having to draw attention to ourselves as individuals. Moreover, even though the habit does not make the monk, it helps to form a monk as he strives to become *interiorly* what he professes to be *outwardly* by his habit.

Many people, with faith and without, come to monasteries to find peace; and the fact that they keep coming back suggests that they find it. A monastery, with its Divine Office, its monks or nuns in habits, speaks to people of God. Shrines like Lourdes or Ars are another kind of icon. Although we live in a secular age, many people go to monasteries and convents, and more and more go on pilgrimage. The BBC did two programmes of 'reality television' on 'The Monastery' and 'The Convent' in which a group of men went for an extended stay to Worth Abbey, and, a year or so later a group of women went to stay in a Poor Clare Convent. Both series were huge hits and have had a lasting impact on many people. A highlight for the people who stayed at Worth Abbey was their visit to Parkminster, a Carthusian Monastery. Is God so real and so important that people are ready to dedicate their whole lives to him alone? The Carthusian community is an icon which poses this question in stark terms by its way of life. When defending our religion we can give the impression that our relationship with God is a means to various other ends, such as the rights and value of the individual person, or the educational and health programmes undertaken by the Church, or its civilizing influence down the ages. The Carthusians witness to us and to the world that God is not a means to an end. Union with God is the supreme good, and everything else, however good in itself, is a means to that end. The Carthusians actually live that truth and challenge us by their way of life to continue our conversion process.

However, each diocese, each parish, even each Catholic family is called to be an icon of Christ. We are called to 'cry out the Gospel with our lives', as Charles de Foucauld put it. As the liturgy is the source and goal of our Christian activity, it must have this iconic quality, not just in the words, not just in theory: people must be able to contemplate with their eyes what they hear with their ears, and the ceremonial and everything to do with the liturgy must point beyond itself to the Mystery that is being celebrated. The celebrant or liturgist knows that Christ wishes to manifest himself through the liturgy and, like the iconographer, he must use his skills to allow this to happen. There is not the time, nor is it the place, for him to indulge in self-expression. Everything must be subordinated to the task of making clear the active presence of Christ and our consequent participation in the Christian Mystery. Icons have several layers of meaning, and so has the Mass. It is not only an external celebration: it is also a spiritual journey, an ascension with Christ into the presence of the Father to be transformed by him as sons and daughters of God, as we travel through conversion to contemplation. Room has to be made within the celebration for that interior journey which is at once both deeply personal and intensely communal. As far as we are concerned, we become icons of Christ to the extent that we cut through the rock of pride to find Christ in our own heart and in other people. The more we find Christ outside of our ego, both beneath it in the depths of the heart and in our neighbour, as well as in the events of everyday life, the more will we manifest Christ to others.

The Church is icon of Christ in each local assembly; but it is also icon of Christ as a world-wide body. As St John Chrysostom said: 'Christ makes a single body. Thus, he who lives in Rome looks on the Indians as his own members. Is there any union to be compared with that?'[2] When God became man, he adopted what was common to all members of the human race by taking our nature, thus healing the divisions in himself that, in the story of the Tower of Babel, had divided humankind into separate groupings. Every time we celebrate the Eucharist we know that we are one with people of every race, nation and class, and we leave behind us all secondary things like nationality in so far as it divides us from other people. The Church as icon of Christ must be the pictorial image of this unity restored. It must be a unity transcending nationality, a unity that we can hear with our ears, touch with our hands, a unity clearly the result of the word of life, a unity that is a revelation of Christ himself. It must be a unity that belongs to the ordinary, human, everyday level. God stooped to that level when he became man, and icons belong to that level, even though they are windows into eternity. It must be a human society and capable of operating as a human society, but a very special kind of society in which each part manifests the whole and the whole knows it is not greater than each part, a society that receives everything that makes it worthwhile from God. We cannot choose between the Eucharistic dimension and the universal dimension of the Church because both belong to its very nature while it is on earth: hence our need for the pope. He can speak for the whole because, like all other bishops and priests, he presides over it each time he celebrates the Eucharist (Eucharistic dimension); but, unlike other individual bishops, he must translate this presidency in the Catholic Eucharist into a truly universal ministry because, as Bishop of Rome, he is heir to the role of St Peter in the Church (universal dimension).

In our relationship with the world outside the visible Church, I believe it is our primary task to find Christ there too; but we will only do so with success if we first find him in our celebration of the Christian Mystery. The more intensely we find him in the Mystery of the Church, the more clearly we will find him everywhere. The icon for our relations with the outside world is Mother Teresa, who loved across frontiers because she found Christ suffering everywhere. However, we are to love, not only those who suffer, but the authentically human wherever it may be. Humanity has been distorted by sin, but it is not entirely corrupt; otherwise God could not have become man. God has taken human nature to himself in the humanity of Jesus Christ. This includes all that is authentically human in other religions as well, and even in the lives of agnostics and atheists. And we are to take up all this and offer it on the paten at the offertory of the Mass, so that it may be united to the self-offering of Christ and thus receive a value it would never have on its own. Hence the Eucharist is both the source of our activity in the world and its goal. While all this involves loving all human beings and everything that is authentically human about them, it is the opposite of the belief that all religions are the same. Christ is the meaning of all things, the reason for creation and the seed of its transformation at the end of time. As Henri de Lubac SJ wrote:

> Catholicism is religion itself. It is the form that humanity must put on in order finally to be itself. It is the only reality which involves by its existence no opposition. It is therefore the very opposite of a 'closed society'.[3]

After Vatican II, too many of us tried to be the same as everybody else; and the world ceased to find us interesting. The more we tried to meet people on their level, the easier they found it to ignore us and our message. We did not realize that our love for them demanded that we should be different; and their interest in us would only come about if we were different. Not that we should try to be different: we should be so united to Christ through the Eucharist that the Holy Spirit can turn us into what we celebrate, icons that manifest Christ's presence in humanity.

The word that expresses what holds together all these different aspects of the Church and levels of our participation in the Christian Mystery is '*synergy*'. Firstly there is the synergy between the operations of the Persons of the Blessed Trinity in the work of salvation; then the synergy between the divine and human wills in Christ; then the synergy between Christ and the Church by the power of the Spirit working in word and sacrament in the liturgy.

Then there is the synergy between the Eucharistic and the universal dimensions of the Church, and the corresponding synergy between the apostolic authority of the local bishop and that of the pope, brought about because Christ works through each in the power of the same Spirit. Finally, there is the growing synergy in the soul of each Christian as he or she becomes more and more *pure in heart*, with more and more of his or her free will being in line with that of Christ, becoming more and more capable of seeing and loving Christ in all the various ways he manifests himself to us, and hence experiencing for himself or herself the unity of the Christian Mystery. This synergy is the work of the Holy Spirit whom we invoke in the epiclesis in every Mass: a small prayer with enormous implications which we have tried to spell out in this book.

Notes

1. Alexander Schmemann, *The World As Sacrament* (Darton, Longman & Todd, 1965), p. 27.
2. John Chrysostom, *Homily* 61, 1 (*PG* 59, 362) quoted from Olivier Clément, *The Roots of Christian Mysticism*, p. 116.
3. Henri de Lubac, *Catholicism*, pp. 156–7.

Printed in the United Kingdom
by Lightning Source UK Ltd.
133428UK00001B/298-423/P